THE ITALIAN TABLE

THE
ITALIAN TABLE

Eating Together For Every Occasion

RON SUHANOSKY

Photography by Alberto Peroli

KYLE BOOKS

Published in 2011 by Kyle Books
www.kylebooks.com

Distributed by National Book Network
4501 Forbes Blvd., Suite 200
Lanham, MD 20706
Phone: (800) 462-6420 Fax: (301) 429-5746
custserv@nbnbooks.com

Text © 2011 Ron Suhanosky
Photography © 2010 Alberto Peroli
Book design © 2010 Kyle Cathie Limited

Project editor: Anja Schmidt
Designer: Jan Derevjanik
Photographer: Alberto Peroli
Food Styling: Rebecca Jurkevitch
Prop Styling: Roy Finamore
Copyeditor: Deborah Weiss Geline
Production: Lisa Pinnell and Gemma John

Library of Congress Control Number:
2011926470

Color reproduction by Scanhouse
Printed and bound in China by C & C Offset

CONTENTS

AT THE TABLE

Family Dining Is What It's All About

My aim with this book is to do the same thing for family dining that I did for pasta in my first book: make a traditional Italian-style approach as accessible, appealing, and delicious as possible for modern home chefs. The principles of family cooking and dining have always been in my blood. They were so fundamental to my *nonne*'s lifestyles and are so ingrained in mine. They were equally fundamental to the success of my restaurants and will continue to be the focus of all my culinary ventures going forward. It's relatively easy to create an ambiance that transports diners to a time and place reminiscent of the Old Country. But that's not necessarily the main goal. What's most important is getting everybody to the table to eat family style—*come in famiglia*. It's about maximizing the family dining experience through sophisticated, stylish, and easy-to-prepare recipes.

If you think about the most successful meals you've had or made, they often take you back to your childhood, back to your grandmother's table, back to those fondly recalled family dinners. When you eat alone or in a hurry, it's about nothing more than refueling and getting right back on the road. But if you make the effort to organize and prepare a real family-style meal, you're preparing for a transcendent experience. The meal becomes so much more than just putting food in your mouth. Almost all the recipes in this book reflect the influence of such family characters as my Italian *nonne* (my great-grandmother and grandmother), my wife, Colleen's grandfather Joe Piazza, and my Hungarian grandmother Irene Suhanosky.

My Familial Influences

My great-grandmother Rose Carbone was who we called Big Nonna. She is the main inspiration for this book. Big Nonna was warm and nurturing. She taught me the fundamentals of Italian family cooking by example. She was most often seen in the kitchen wearing her housecoat. My grandmother Rachel Gaudino absorbed all of her mother, Rose's know-how and added some sophistication. She carried on the family traditions with a more modern, elegant twist. I represent the third generation to uphold those traditions, adding my own spin to the recipes, taking them to the next level. (Meanwhile, the tables have stayed the same.) A good example is my Caprese salad, where I take the three traditional ingredients—buffalo mozzarella, fresh tomatoes, and basil—and add sliced watermelon and pesto, making the dish simultaneously lighter (courtesy of the watermelon), more complex, and zestier (thanks to the pesto). Other examples might include adding strawberries and aged balsamic vinegar to a traditional San Marzano tomato sauce—a signature dish at my restaurants that was featured in my first book—or the Roasted Wild Boar with Sweet Potato Puree, *Mostarda*, and Grated Bittersweet Chocolate, a dinner-party dish with Renaissance overtones that we introduce in this book. Thanks to Big Nonna, I knew I wanted to be a chef from a very young age—probably about eight years old. I wasn't exactly like the kid who sees a fireman or an astronaut and says, "That's what I want to be when I grow up." Big Nonna instilled in me such a strong sense of comfort in her old kitchen on Farren Avenue in New Haven that I said to myself, "I want that. I want to be happy like Big Nonna." Of course it took me a while to articulate a career path, going to cooking school, doing *stages* in Italy, and eventually opening my own family restaurant. But I knew very early that the way to capture the happiness I felt from Big Nonna was to learn to do all the things she did in the kitchen.

I was the first-born and only son in the family. Both of Big Nonna's sons were killed in World War II, and in my generation the other kids were girls—my sisters. In Big Nonna's eyes, I was the little prince. Under normal circumstances, kids are kept away from the dangers of a kitchen—the stove, the flames, the knives. Big Nonna took me under the skirts of her apron and put me at ease with all of this. I could tell she enjoyed having me around as her pint-size assistant. (My son, Roman, is in a similar position.) She taught me it is OK to stick your finger (very quickly) in a pot of boiling pasta water in order to taste and make sure the water is properly salted. I have raised all three of my kids to feel equally comfortable in the kitchen. I've taught them how to avoid getting hurt, how not to be afraid, and I've shown them my livelihood. Hopefully that's how our family cooking traditions will be carried on. Because of all that Big Nonna taught me, even though she's not around anymore to nurture my kids, I feel there's a direct link from her to them.

My Geographical Influences

The Italian side of Colleen's family is Sicilian; the Italian side of mine is from Campania. So we start off with a nice regional mix. Colleen and I have cooked in Tuscany, Umbria, and Piedmont, adding to that mix. We've traveled throughout Italy, always seeking to soak up other regional influences. And, of course, there's an American take on many things Italian in the kitchen—from the very traditional Italian-American dishes Big Nonna used to cook, to a more modern approach like Grandmother Rose's, and then on to the more eclectic twenty-first century style featured at my restaurants.

In addition to my mother's Italian roots, there are my dad's Polish and Hungarian ones. Sunday family gatherings were generally for the Italian side, while Saturdays we would get together with the Polish-Hungarian side. My father's mother, Grandmother Irene, would make dishes like chicken paprikash from her native Hungary, and a lot of preparations with pork and kielbasa sausage. She also did lots of baking with phyllo. Many of the things she did with kielbasa, I now do with sweet sausage or some other

Italian ingredient. Her influence on my cooking was not as heavy in terms of actual recipes, but she definitely instilled in me a love for pork and fueled my desire to explore various interesting uses of it within my own style. My recipe for Caramelized Brussels Sprouts with Crispy Guanciale, presented in chapter six of this book, is an example.

Simplicity and Tradition

As I said, the main purpose of this book is to bring families to the table together. Naturally, under the heading "families," we include the nuclear unit—parents plus kids—but also the extended one, with aunts, uncles, cousins, in-laws, step-siblings, grown-ups and kids of all ages, and of course anybody who may not be a blood relative but who is "just like family." The recipes reflect this spirit of inclusion; they may serve four to six for everyday family dinners, six to eight for when company is expected, or much larger groups for weekend parties.

For me, a great recipe almost always has a traditional foundation. It has relatively few ingredients and it looks for good complements and contrasts of flavors and textures to achieve a delicious balance. My cooking style starts with basic principles and fundamental recipes, a light-handed approach, and a willingness to add the occasional adventurous or quirky spin on them. If I had to label my style, I would call it modern American with an Italian accent and some Eastern European influences.

I think there is a misconception that Italian cooking relies on a large number of ingredients and heavy seasonings. Actually, the simpler the better. Italians understand how to use their ingredients properly. It's all about restraint. If you make a nice fresh tomato sauce for your pasta, then load it up with a ton of garlic because that's what you think makes it authentically Italian—Italians cook with a lot of garlic, right?—it doesn't work. All you really need is a touch of garlic to achieve that perfect balance. My favorite Italian dishes have three to five ingredients and they use them as seasoning agents, rather than including a lot of spices or relying on long grocery lists or complicated instructions. If you have sweet flavors and need some salt for balance, you simply add anchovies, capers, or perhaps a bit of salty grated cheese—just a touch, for seasoning.When I'm creating new recipes, I try to incorporate the best of my family traditions—those old-style dishes from my grandmothers. I also like to experiment with an even older tradition, the ancient medieval and Renaissance practice of combining sweet and savory flavors. It's another route to that all-important balance. Braised baccalà in a tomato sauce, for example, would have been very familiar to my Italian grandmothers. Adding prunes might have seemed crazy to them. But I found it's a great flavor enhancement and a fun way to expand modern family palates.

Every Recipe Starts at the Table

Every recipe starts at the table. This is my "Call me Ishmael." What do I mean? It all starts with a clear concept or vision of the meal. You've got to picture how the table will be set, who will be sitting there, when and how the food will be served. The food itself is the centerpiece of something bigger, which is a warm family gathering over hearty, delicious dishes enjoyed at a leisurely pace. All the various characters from several generations take time to enjoy one another's company, drawing sustenance from the food and psychic energy from the communal spirit. First, you have to know who you're cooking for and why. From there, you figure out what they want to eat. You work your way back, assembling the menu and choosing the dishes based on the occasion and seasonally available ingredients.

Just as my own personal and professional development as a chef was inspired by many real-life family characters, almost every one of my formative food experiences is symbolized in my mind's eye by a particular table—the first of which is Big Nonna's. As a restaurateur, I very consciously re-created specific dining scenarios by using actual tables from various family homes. Each table has its own character. It sparks conversations, tells stories, evokes memories. Each represents at least one aspect of my family's cooking and dining lore, and seven of them are used to set the tone for each of the chapters of this book.

All of this book's recipes are master recipes in the sense that they are not only scalable (that is, expandable for larger family groups) but flexible in terms of components that can be used to create variations. Many of them were devised with an eye toward reconstituting them as leftovers. Both of these are essential features of family-style cooking. It's exciting to me to cook just enough food so we eat everything fresh, but I know that's not always the way it works with a family. Since most families are on a budget, it's nice to be economical and get a couple of different meals out of a dish. Exercising frugality by coming up with clever variations and ways to reinvent leftovers was second nature in our immigrant families. None of our family members who came over from the Old Country—whether it was Italy, Poland, or Hungary—were rich. They all took pride in getting the most out of what they had.

In the spirit of *The Italian Table*, I encourage you to do the same. Use these recipes to bring your family back to the table so everyone can eat happily together. *Buon apetito!*

—*Ron Suhanosky*

THE PANTRY

Following is a list of ingredients that are called for in the recipes contained in this book, or are ones I tend to keep around because of their high degree of usefulness.

AMARETTI—These macaroon-type cookies, made from almonds, egg whites, and sugar, are crunchy on the outside and soft within when fresh-baked. The most common brand is Lazzaroni's Amaretti di Saronno, which come in pairs, enclosed in a printed tissue-paper wrapper, inside a red tin. Once they've been shipped to stores and sold, they are generally quite hard and crunchy. In this form, they lend themselves to being crushed and used as a garnish or an ingredient for added texture. They add sweet and mildly bitter almond flavors.

ANCHOVIES—I employ anchovies frequently as a seasoning agent to add salt. They should be added sparingly, especially in combination with milder ingredients. I prefer the salt-cured anchovies that come in sealed glass jars or are sold loose (by weight) at Italian groceries. They should be thoroughly rinsed and patted dry and their bones pulled out before using. I hesitate to use the fillets that come in olive oil because I feel they have other marinated, vinegary flavors, whereas the bone-in, salt-cured type retains a purer, more concentrated anchovy flavor.

BALSAMIC VINEGAR—This is not vinegar in the usual sense of the word: It's made from Trebbiano grape juice, reduced and aged at least eight years in wooden casks according to an ancient, traditional formula. The genuine name-protected product comes from two regions: the city of Modena and the province of Reggio-Emilia. There are many commercial, imitation balsamic vinegars of varying quality. For a recipe ingredient, I always use an 8-year-old authentic version. For drizzling as a garnish or in dressings, I might use a more expensive, longer-aged (12-, 15-, or even 25-year-old) one. Store it in the sealed glass bottle in a cool, dry place.

BLACK PEPPERCORNS—My pepper grinder always contains black peppercorns, which I use along with salt to season all preparations. In Italy, they never use white pepper because it's considered too fragrant for most recipes, and they hold a similar opinion of black pepper. I have no such qualms about black pepper as long as it's used in proper moderation.

BREAD CRUMBS—I keep stale bread wrapped in a brown paper bag so I can toast it and grind it up in a food processor to make bread crumbs. If you buy dry bread crumbs, I suggest unseasoned ones so you can add your own seasonings as per the recipe.

CAPERS—My preference is for the salt-cured capers; be sure to rinse them well before using.

CHOCOLATE (BITTERSWEET)—Caillebaut bittersweet chocolate (70% cacao) is my standard. Store the open package in the fridge.

CORNMEAL—I recommend course, stone-ground cornmeal (organic if possible) for multiple uses, including making polenta. Store it just like flour in a sealed container in a cool, dry place.

DRIED FRUITS—I like to keep a variety of dried fruits around—raisins (black and golden), prunes, currants, and perhaps even apricots—to provide a sweet balance in some of my savory sauces. Dried fruits keep their shape when braised and offer nicely concentrated flavors. Store them in a sealed container or resealable plastic bag in a cool, dry place.

EXTRA VIRGIN OLIVE OIL—This is the first cold-pressed, unprocessed, unfiltered product of green olives. It comes from various countries around the Mediterranean and also from California. Extra virgin olive oil is dense and fruity in flavor, and is therefore appropriate as a dressing or garnish, but not for cooking (for which I use grapeseed oil). I prefer a high-quality extra virgin oil from southern Italy. The northern production zones, particularly Tuscany, tend to produce oil that is too peppery for my taste. Store in a sealed bottle in a dark place at room temperature for months. See also "olive oil."

FLOUR—King Arthur all-purpose is my pantry choice for regular wheat flour. Rice flour is also good to have on hand. It's finer, holds the least amount of moisture, and works well for dusting as well as for coating for sautéeing and frying. Keep all flours in airtight containers in a cool, dry place.

GRAPESEED OIL—This is the oil I use most in cooking because of its useful properties: It has a high smoke point (over 400°F), which makes it good for sautéing and frying, and is neutral-tasting, which means it does not interfere with other ingredient flavors. It can also be stored at room temperature, unlike some other oils, which need refrigeration to prevent them from becoming rancid.

KOSHER SALT—I always use only kosher salt because its relatively large, soft, triangular crystals are easy to see as you put them on the food and they adhere, dissolve, and mix well at either the ingredient or final seasoning stage.

NUTS—Almonds, hazelnuts, pistachios, walnuts, and pine nuts find their way into many of my recipes for their flavors and textures. I always toast them beforehand to bring out their best flavor, shelling them and making sure to remove whatever husk or skin is on the nut itself. Keep them in the refrigerator or in a tightly sealed, airtight container so they do not become rancid.

OLIVE OIL—All of my recipes specify either "extra virgin olive oil" or simply "olive oil." The latter is often referred to on its labels as "pure olive oil" or "light olive oil." It is filtered, less dense, and has a lighter, yellower color and higher smoke point than extra virgin, making it appropriate for cooking. See also "extra virgin olive oil."

PARMIGIANO-REGGIANO—Genuine Parmigiano-Reggiano, a name-protected product from designated areas of Reggio-Emilia, is one of the world's greatest cheeses, prized for its complex, nutty flavors and crystalline moist-yet-dry texture. Grated, it is used as a garnish or thickening/enriching ingredient. Authentic Grana Padano, also name-protected but from a wider production zone with less stringent rules, is a less-expensive alternative.

(HOT) RED PEPPER FLAKES—These dried seeds of the pepper plant, also known as peperoncini, can be stored like spices in a cool, dark place in an airtight container for months. They are used to provide spicy hotness when you don't want the fragrance of cracked black pepper.

RICE—There are three main varieties of Italian risotto rice that I recommend (in descending order of quality): Vialone Nano, Carnaroli, and Arborio. I prefer Carnaroli for most preparations. If risotto is the main course or focus, use the more costly Vialone Nano. Arborio is ranked third because its grains are not as sturdy. One of the main criteria for risotto is that the rice grains release their starch gradually while retaining their shape and not breaking up.

SALT—See "kosher salt."

SPICES—I usually keep the following spices around: aniseed, bay leaves, fennel pollen and fennel seed. The rest I buy as needed.

VINEGAR—In addition to balsamic vinegar, which I consider a product apart, I usually keep around some white vinegar, red wine vinegar, and cider vinegar. White vinegar is used for brining or any time I don't want discoloration. Red wine vinegar is for raw preparations—mainly salad dressings—whereas cider vinegar is used as a flavoring ingredient in cooked dishes.

SAN MARZANO TOMATOES—These are another of Italy's most prized name-protected products, grown in the part of Campania around the town of San Marzano, near Naples. They are vine-ripened, canned whole in their own juices, and shipped all over the world. Even when a recipe calls for pureed tomatoes, I always recommend starting with whole San Marzanos because they have a better flavor. Other types of canned organic plum tomatoes may be substituted, but San Marzano sets the highest standard. Fresh local plum tomatoes can also be substituted, but they must be perfectly ripe, which is rare to find.

~1~

JUST US

Weekday Dinners for the Family

{SERVING 4 TO 6}

OVERLEAF: Veal Scallopine with Artichokes and Toasted Pistachios (page 24).

Our Swift Table

Thinking back to all the times I sat at my mom's, my grandmother Little Nonna's, and my great-grandmother Big Nonna's tables throughout my childhood, it's great to know that now I have my own table where my kids can sit and create their family traditions. Our table is a Stephen Swift creation that will no doubt be passed down and become a family heirloom, just as my great-grandmother's and grandmother's tables have been. Swift was an artisan woodcarver and furniture-maker on Nantucket, and I was lucky enough to find my rare signed original at a yard sale. It was the centerpiece of the dining area in our home on Folger Avenue, Nantucket, and became, for me, a wonderful symbol of our family's roots on the island, which our kids will always cherish.

Swift tables are made according to five designs (cross-leg, tapered leg, pedestal, curved-edge trestle, and straight-edge trestle); mine is a tapered leg. For each table, wood colors and grains are carefully matched, and the most exceptional boards are specially selected for the tops. Chair spacing is carefully measured and planned according to the client's needs. The bases are designed for function as well as appearance, the craftsmanship is unparalleled, and the result is a unique, timeless piece made to last generations.

This chapter presents the core essence of this book, which is the smaller family unit getting together around the table for dinner, a ritual that is so central in the day-to-day life of the Italian culture. In my family growing up, and in the family I created as a grownup, there is always that spirit of togetherness and participation. In today's busy culture, it doesn't always come so naturally. So it helps if you have a repertoire of reliable, delicious recipes that are quick and easy to prepare.

These are recipes that I prepare during the week to serve four to six people at our Swift table. They are meant for those regular occasions, when everybody is eager to come together at the end of the day for some delicious food. Among them are several "go-to" dishes, those all-time family favorites to which I add a flavor-enhancing twist of the kind that can make everyday dinners much more interesting—the veal scaloppine recipe on page 24, for example. This chapter also features two everyday family staples, fish and chicken, presented by way of two different sophisticated yet easily applicable cooking methods—*al cartoccio* (in a packet) and *al mattone* (under a brick)—that bring out the best in their main ingredients. They were proven and highly popular dishes in our family-style restaurants, and they will serve you equally well in your home kitchen.

COLLEEN'S SCHIACCIATA

SERVES 4 TO 6

275 milliliters warm water
(approximately 1¼ cups)

1 teaspoon active dry yeast

3 cups all-purpose flour, plus
more for adding to dough,
flouring work surface,
and dusting loaf

2 teaspoons kosher salt

extra virgin olive oil, approximately
3 tablespoons

sea salt

Colleen and the kids spent the entire school year of 2009-10 in Italy, living near the center of Florence, in an apartment off the Piazza San Marco. She worked occasionally at a bakery in the neighborhood, and this recipe is her adaptation of a typical local *schiacciata* (pronounced "skee-ah-CHA-tah"). It quickly became one of our kids' favorite after-school snacks. The verb *schiacciare* means to "squash" or "flatten." Therefore, a *schiacciata* is something that's been flattened—exactly what you do with the dough to make this bread. I think of it as a thinner, crustier version of foccacia. It's seasoned simply, with nothing more than some good extra virgin olive oil and salt, and works really well in place of crackers as an accompaniment to *antipasti*. Most bakers use their fingers to create dimples in the surface of the dough so it can collect and absorb tiny pools of the drizzled olive oil as it bakes.

TIMING NOTE: The dough has two resting/rising periods of up to 2 hours each

1. Combine the water and yeast and stir until thoroughly dissolved. Mix and mound the flour and salt in a large mixing bowl and make a well at the top. Using a wooden spoon, stir in the yeast mixture until a sticky, wet dough is formed. It should be too sticky to knead on a board but dry enough to separate from the bowl when stirred. If it is too wet, fold in more flour, 1 to 2 tablespoons at a time, and mix for 10 minutes, until it becomes shiny and pulls away easily from the bowl. Note: The dough can also be made with an electric mixer, using the paddle attachment, on medium speed.

2. Coat the inside of a large bowl with olive oil, place the dough in the bowl, cover with a thin kitchen towel, and let rest at room temperature (with no significant light or heat sources) until doubled in volume, 1 to 2 hours.

3. Place the dough on a well-floured work surface; stretch and flatten it into a 8 x 12-inch rectangle, about 1 inch thick. Sprinkle with flour and, using both hands, carefully turn it over so as not to stretch or bend it, then sprinkle the other side with flour. Place the dough on an ungreased 9 x 13-inch sheet pan. Use your fingers to dimple the surface of the dough about an inch apart. Place the pan in a draft-free area—an unlit oven is ideal—and let rise until doubled in bulk, 1 to 2 hours.

4. Remove the sheet pan from the oven and preheat the oven to 425°F.

5. Dimple the surface of the dough again, drizzle generously with olive oil, and sprinkle with sea salt. Bake for 10 to 15 minutes, or until golden. Transfer to a cutting board, drizzle with olive oil, sprinkle with sea salt, cut into squares, and serve hot.

STORAGE: The bread will stay fresh in a bread box at room temperature for 2 days; wrapped tightly in plastic and/or sealed in a freezer-proof plastic bag, it can be stored in the freezer for up to 2 weeks.

PAPPA AL POMODORO

SERVES 4 TO 6

1 large loaf stale Italian bread,
cut into 3-inch squares

2 cups carrots, cut into 1-inch
pieces (from 1 large or
2 medium carrots)

2 cups Spanish onion, cut into
1-inch cubes (from 1 medium
onion)

2 cups celery, cut into 1-inch
pieces (from 1 large or
2 medium stalks)

2 tablespoons grapeseed oil

1 garlic clove

two 28-ounce cans San Marzano
tomatoes

about 4 cups water

½ cup (tightly packed) fresh
basil leaves

kosher salt and cracked black
pepper

about 6 tablespoons extra virgin
olive oil

4 to 6 tablespoons grated
Parmigiano-Reggiano

This is a traditional Tuscan summer soup, simmered but served at room temperature. I first came across it when I worked at Il Cibrèo in Florence, and I couldn't stop eating it. The word *pappa* means "pap" or "mush," as in baby food; it comes from the Latin root for eating with gusto, which is one of the reasons this is an ideal family recipe for a first course or lunch, and a great way to get kids to eat their vegetables.

INGREDIENT NOTES: With this version, I call for canned San Marzano tomatoes because it can be difficult to find consistently ripe tomatoes year-round. When it's the dead of summer, though, and the local tomatoes are perfectly ripe and juicy, use fresh ones. The bread, tomato, and olive oil combination is fundamental and supremely delicious. Using the best-quality extra virgin olive oil for the garnish is key. Another crucial component is the bread: It should be a good rustic-style bread that is definitely stale—dry and hard, but of course not moldy—so that when it's toasted and then simmered, it melds completely with the tomatoes to make this soup true to form: smooth, hearty, and irresistible.

1. Preheat the oven to 400°F. Toast the stale bread in the oven until lightly golden in color, about 5 minutes. Set aside to cool.

2. Place the carrots, onions, and celery in the bowl of a food processor and process for 2 to 3 minutes, or until finely chopped.

3. Place the grapeseed oil in a 5-quart heavy-bottomed saucepan over medium heat. Add the carrot mixture and cook for 4 to 6 minutes, or until translucent. Add the garlic, tomatoes (and their juices), and enough water to cover. Raise the heat, bring to a boil, then lower the heat to a simmer. Add the toasted bread, making sure it is completely submerged. Add the basil and simmer for about 1 hour, stirring regularly. The soup will turn a rich red color, and the bread will melt into the tomatoes.

4. Pass the soup through a food mill into a serving container large enough to hold the entire amount (alternatively, use a stand or immersion blender). Season with salt and pepper and let the soup come to room temperature. Serve in shallow bowls with a drizzle of about 1 tablespoon extra virgin olive oil and a sprinkle of grated Parmigiano-Reggiano per serving.

TUSCAN KALE WITH SHAVED PEARS AND CRUSHED AMARETTI

SERVES 4 TO 6

1 tablespoon balsamic vinegar

2 tablespoons extra virgin olive oil

2 bunches Tuscan (or black) kale, washed and trimmed, stems removed

3 packages amaretti (6 cookies), crushed

1 ripe medium Anjou pear, washed

¼ cup grated pecorino Romano

kosher salt and cracked black pepper

I had never thought about eating uncooked kale until a few years ago, when the raw food diet trend started to spike, and Colleen convinced me to try it. I did some investigation and discovered there was something of a tradition of making salads with raw Tuscan kale in Italy. Much to my delight, this was also an opportunity to put together a couple of very interesting complementary and contrasting textures and flavors—the peppery, slightly bitter greens with their bubble-shaped leaves and fresh crunch, alongside the mildly bittersweet and very crunchy *amaretti*, and the sweet, ripe pears.

INGREDIENT NOTES: *Amaretti* are crunchy almond macaroons, best known worldwide by the Lazzarroni brand Amaretti di Saronno (Saronno being a town in Lombardy). They come in a signature red tin, pairs of little nuggets wrapped in printed, colored tissue paper. *Amaretti*, literally translated, means "small bitter things." They start out crispy on the outside and chewy inside; the store-bought kind are usually hard and crunchy by the time they get to us. Although conventionally served as dessert cookies with ice cream or coffee, they've always been one of my favorite prepared ingredients to provide crunch and flavor accents to savory recipes. Black kale, aka Tuscan (or Lacinato or dinosaur) is called *cavolo nero* in Italian, literally "black cabbage," since it is technically a member of the cabbage family.

1. Place the balsamic vinegar and olive oil in a large stainless-steel bowl. Add the kale and amaretti.

2. Using a sharp knife or mandoline, slice the pear thin (⅛-inch slices), removing the seeds, and add to the bowl.

3. Add the pecorino Romano and toss thoroughly so the vinaigrette coats the kale well. Season to taste with salt and pepper, and serve in a ceramic (or other non-reactive) bowl.

VEAL SCALOPPINE WITH ARTICHOKES AND TOASTED PISTACHIOS

SERVES 4 TO 6

4 medium artichokes

3 lemons, cut in half

½ cup shelled unsalted
pistachios

3 pounds veal scaloppine
(twelve 4-ounce cutlets,
about 3 x 5 inches and
½ inch thick each)

1 cup rice flour

2 tablespoons kosher salt, plus
more to taste

1 tablespoon cracked black
pepper, plus more to taste

3 large brown eggs

4 tablespoons grapeseed oil

1 cup dry white wine

On the way to the VinItaly wine convention in Verona a couple of years ago, I made an extended stop in Milan, where I had several excellent versions of the classic veal scaloppine alla Milanese. I daydreamed about these dishes almost the entire flight back and was determined to create my own variation, with a twist. I started working on this recipe as soon as I got home, introducing the combination of toasted pistachios, probably my favorite ingredient among all nuts, and artichokes. The cooking procedure involves a dredging in rice flour, which is fine textured and light, and a minimal coating of egg before sautéing to a golden brown color. In the sauce, the unique, subtle flavor of artichokes works really well with that of the toasted nuts, which add a nice texture contrast.

INGREDIENT NOTE: Most supermarkets and butcher shops offer prepared veal scaloppine—and chicken, too, if you prefer that as a substitute. But feel free to do it the old-fashioned way, like my grandmothers did: Buy veal sirloin, take it home, and pound it into *scallopine* with the wooden meat pounder.

TIMING NOTE: The main prep stages involve trimming the artichokes, which should be left in ice-cold lemon water until ready to cook, and toasting the pistachios.

1. First prepare the artichokes: Add the juice of 1 lemon to a large bowl of ice water. Working with one artichoke at a time, cut off and discard the stem. Snap off and discard the tough, dark green outer leaves. Use a very sharp knife to cut off the tops of the remaining leaves (with the thorns) and discard. Cut the artichoke in half, scrape out and discard the fuzzy choke in the middle, and place the artichoke immediately into the lemon ice water to avoid discoloration. Repeat the procedure with the remaining artichokes, leaving them in the water until ready to cook.

2. Peel the thin husks off the pistachios. Place a cast-iron skillet over medium heat. When the skillet is hot, add the pistachios in one layer. Toast, stirring and tossing regularly, for about 5 minutes, until lightly browned and fragrant. Roughly chop the toasted nuts and set them aside until ready to use.

3. Place the artichokes and the remaining 2 halved lemons, submerged in water by at least 2 inches, in a large saucepan over medium-high heat. Bring to a boil, adjust the heat to maintain a steady simmer, and cook for about 20 minutes, or until the artichokes are fork tender on the outside. Slice the artichokes lengthwise ½-inch thick and set aside.

4. Place the rice flour in a shallow bowl. Pat the scaloppine dry and season both sides with the salt and pepper, then dredge them in the rice flour and set aside.

5. Crack the eggs into a large mixing bowl and lightly beat. Spread a double layer of paper towels over a large plate or platter.

6. Place the grapeseed oil in a large skillet over medium heat. Dip each floured piece of veal in the egg until it is completely submerged and lightly coated. Working in batches, sauté the scaloppine until lightly golden in color, 2 to 3 minutes on each side. (Give each piece enough room, about 1 inch all around, so they are not crowded or touching.) When done, place the scaloppine on the paper towel to absorb any excess grease; add additional layers of paper towel as necessary.

7. Add the artichoke slices and pistachios to the pan and sauté for 4 to 6 minutes, then transfer to a plate. Deglaze the pan with the white wine and cook until reduced by half. Season the pan sauce with salt and pepper.

8. Place the scaloppine on a platter with the artichoke slices and pistachios on top, drizzle with the pan sauces, and serve hot.

WHOLE ROASTED CAULIFLOWER IN OLIVE OIL WITH SPICES

SERVES 4 TO 6

1 head cauliflower, left whole, trimmed and washed

2 tablespoons olive oil

¼ teaspoon ground nutmeg

⅛ teaspoon ground cloves

1 teaspoon kosher salt

½ teaspoon cracked black pepper

I find that roasting most foods whole—including vegetables—allows for more of their inherent flavors to be retained within, as opposed to cooking them in pieces where they take on more of the "outside" flavors from other ingredients in the recipe. This cauliflower recipe is the perfect illustration. It's quick, simple, and highlights the cauliflower's essential flavors. I love to serve it as a side dish for roasted chicken or uncomplicated fish dishes.

1. Preheat the oven to 350°F.

2. Place the cauliflower in a medium ovenproof glass casserole. Pour the olive oil on top, making sure the entire head is lightly coated. Season with the nutmeg, cloves, salt, and pepper. Cover loosely with aluminum foil and place in the oven for 45 to 60 minutes, or until fork tender. The cauliflower should begin to take on some color and also become translucent in its stem.

3. Cut the head into six equal portions, arrange on a platter, and serve hot.

SHRIMP SCAMPI WITH PANE GRATUGIATTA, CHICKPEA PUREE, AND SAUTÉED ESCAROLE

SERVES 4 TO 6

4 teaspoons unsalted butter

3 pounds large (U10) shrimp, peeled and deveined

1 tablespoon kosher salt

½ tablespoon cracked black pepper

1 garlic clove, finely chopped

½ cup chopped fresh Italian (flat-leaf) parsley

½ cup dried unseasoned bread crumbs

¼ cup fresh lemon juice (from 1 to 2 medium lemons)

Chickpea Puree (page 30)

Sauteed Escarole (page 30)

I have always enjoyed bringing traditional Italian dishes back to life in a modern context. This scampi recipe is the perfect example. There is nothing quite like the Italian-American combination of shrimp, brown butter, garlic, and bread crumbs. It makes a great main dish and is one of the more popular (and best-selling) dishes in Italian restaurants everywhere. With that in mind, I created this version at my place in Nantucket, adding the chickpea puree and sautéed escarole, quickly transforming it into a complete one-plate family meal.

INGREDIENT NOTE: In the United States, the term *scampi* has long been used to refer to large shrimp that are most often served butterflied and buttered then grilled, broiled, or sautéed. Shrimp are generally classified by size as either small, medium, large, or jumbo. The jumbo category is usually labeled U10, meaning less than 10 of them makes up 1 pound. You may also come across extra jumbo or colossal, which are often called *prawns,* though technically prawns are a different species. For this recipe, I prefer to use the jumbo size.

TIMING NOTE: Prepare the chickpea puree beforehand so it's ready to serve under the scampi.

1. Place the butter in a large 12-inch skillet over medium heat and melt until lightly golden, 4 to 6 minutes. Season the shrimp with the salt and pepper, and place them in the skillet so they lie flat. Cook until lightly browned, 2 to 3 minutes per side.

2. Add the garlic, parsley, and bread crumbs. Continue to cook over medium heat, stirring occasionally, for 2 to 4 minute. Add the lemon juice and stir to combine.

3. Place equal portions of Chickpea Puree on each plate, top with sautéed scampi, and serve with Sautéed Escarole on the side.

Chickpea Puree

1 pound dried chickpeas

1 garlic clove

2 tablespoons olive oil

¼ cup fresh lemon juice (from
    1 to 2 medium lemons)

kosher salt and cracked black
    pepper

INGREDIENT NOTE: I strongly prefer to start with dried chickpeas to make this puree; their essential flavors just seem much more delicious and pronounced. If you want to use precooked or canned chickpeas, that's fine, but consider taking the extra step instead.

TIMING NOTE: When using dried chickpeas, either soak them in water for 24 hours in advance or follow the "quick soak" procedure in step 1.

1. Place the chickpeas in a saucepot large enough to hold the entire quantity plus enough water to cover by 2 inches. Add the water, bring to a boil over high heat, and cook for 3 to 4 minutes. Cover the pot, remove it from the heat, and set aside for 1 hour. When ready to cook, drain the chickpeas. Skip this step if soaking chickpeas overnight or using canned or precooked chickpeas.

2. Place the chickpeas and garlic in the bowl of a food processor with the blade attachment and process for 1 to 2 minutes, adding the olive oil and lemon juice, until completely pureed. Adjust to your desired consistency, adding some cold water if necessary. Season with salt and pepper, and set aside in a covered container at room temperature until ready to serve.

STORAGE: The puree can be stored in a covered container in the fridge for up to 2 weeks.

Sautéed Escarole

2 tablespoons grapeseed oil

1 garlic clove, thinly sliced

1 head escarole, washed,
    dried, core removed, leaves
    separated and roughly
    chopped

kosher salt and cracked black
    pepper

¼ cup fresh lemon juice (from
    1 to 2 medium lemons)

PLACE THE GRAPESEED oil in a large 12-inch skillet over medium heat. Add the garlic and cook until lightly colored around the edges, about 1 minute. Add the escarole and sauté, stirring regularly, until wilted, 5 to 7 minutes. Season with salt and pepper, stir in the lemon juice, and serve as a side dish.

GREEN BEANS IN TONNATO

SERVES 4 TO 6

2 pounds green beans, washed
and trimmed

2 tablespoons kosher salt

FOR THE *TONNATO* SAUCE

16 ounces jarred Italian tuna in oil

¼ cup capers, rinsed and
drained

2 anchovy fillets

¼ cup finely chopped fresh
Italian (flat-leaf) parsley

1 garlic clove

1 cup olive oil

¼ cup fresh lemon juice (from
1 to 2 medium lemons)

kosher salt and cracked black
pepper

Vitello tonnato is one of Italy's most famous and beloved recipes. Featuring the intriguing combination of tender but relatively bland-tasting veal meat with a dynamic tuna-flavored sauce, it is served at room temperature. A classic and versatile hot-weather dish, it is suitable as an appetizer, main course, or side dish for sit-down dinners, buffets, and large parties. Most experts place its origins in Piedmont, some in Venice; in any case, it would be very rare to find an Italian home chef who doesn't have his or her own version. Nowadays, the sauce sometimes comes to resemble a mayonnaise flavored with tuna and capers. I prefer a more traditional approach and have always liked the idea of dressing vegetables with it. A tart, moderately salty sauce, with just the right hint of tuna taste, is such a great way to liven up and balance a mild, somewhat sweet ingredient like these green beans. I've also had great success applying this sauce to fresh ripe tomatoes and even roasted eggplant.

INGREDIENT NOTE: To make the *tonnato* sauce, I prefer imported Italian tuna jarred in oil. The best-quality choices are labeled *ventresca*, which indicates the tasty belly cut, and can be found in gourmet specialty markets, Italian groceries, and (increasingly) supermarkets.

1. First prepare the beans: Fill a large pot with water, add a handful (about 2 heaping tablespoons) of salt, and bring to a boil over high heat. Add the green beans and blanch for 2 minutes. Drain the beans and plunge them into a large pot of ice water to cool. The beans should be barely cooked through and toothsome.

2. To make the sauce, place the tuna, capers, anchovies, parsley, and garlic in a blender and blend on medium speed. Gradually add the olive oil, followed by the lemon juice, continuing to blend until the mixture achieves the consistency of a medium-thick puree. If necessary, thin the puree by adding some cold water. Season with salt and pepper. Toss with the green beans and serve.

FISH AL CARTOCCIO

SERVES 4 TO 6

4 pounds fillets of white-fleshed
   fish, such as sea bass, striper,
   or snapper, skin on (twelve
   4-ounce pieces, about
   3 x 3 inches each)

2 tablespoons kosher salt

1 tablespoon cracked black
   pepper

1 fennel bulb, trimmed and
   thinly sliced (¼ inch thick)
   lengthwise

12 slices lemon, ¼ inch thick,
   seeds removed

½ pound pitted black olives,
   roughly chopped

½ cup (tightly packed) fresh
   Italian (flat-leaf) parsley leaves

½ cup extra virgin olive oil

One of the biggest disappointments faced by home chefs is when their fish gets overcooked and dry. Baking fish in sealed packets is one foolproof solution to this dilemma. I experienced the traditional Italian way of doing this when I did a three-month *stage* at Chef Fabio Picchi's Il Cibrèo restaurant in Florence. I learned a lot of the very old, traditional techniques of Florentine cooking and was also inspired by Picchi's quirky personality. He made lamb brains *al cartoccio* and it was actually quite a popular dish. The summer I cooked in Umbria, I saw whole trout cooked *al cartoccio,* in a large wood-burning oven. Putting those two ideas together when I went back to Nantucket, I came up with this treatment for fish fillets. Not only does it keep your fish moist but it stops the flavors from escaping during the cooking process. When you bring the packets to the table to open them and serve the fish, it's all there, nothing is lost. Different chefs have different methods for folding the packets; I like to snug the top of them by holding the two edges together and making a repeated crimping-type fold, then sealing the ends with a twist that's turned up to hold it tight. This gives the packets a festive air, like little gift packages wrapped up in ribbon.

INGREDIENT NOTE: For this preparation, I like to use 3- to 4-ounce fillets of fish with the skin left on. I use 2 fillets per packet, which equals 1 large whole fish (or 2 small to medium fish) per recipe of this size.

1. Preheat the oven to 400°F.

2. Place a fish fillet, skin side down, in the center of a piece of parchment paper. Season with a pinch each of salt and pepper. Place 1 fennel slice, 2 lemon slices, 3 or 4 olive pieces, and 3 or 4 parsley leaves on top of the fillet and drizzle with about 1 teaspoon of the olive oil. Season another fillet with a pinch each of salt and pepper and lay it on top of the first one, skin side up.

3. To fold the fish packet, bring the longer edges of the paper together above the fillets. Holding the edges together, make a 1-inch fold downward, doubling the bottom edge over the top one. Continue folding in this manner, doubling the folded edges down, until the paper is fairly snug on top of the fillets. Smooth the packet down to the right and left sides of the fillets. Then give each side a firm, full twist to pinch and secure the packet at both ends. Pull the left and right twisted ends up to seal the packet. Repeat steps 1 and 2 until you have 6 packets.

4. Place the fish packets on a baking sheet and bake in the oven for about 30 minutes, until the parchment is slightly golden brown around the edges. Place each fish packet on a plate, serve, and open at the table, taking care with the escaping steam as the packets are opened.

BEETS WITH MINT DRESSING

SERVES 4 TO 6

3 pounds medium beets

2 pounds kosher salt

½ cup (tightly packed) fresh mint
    leaves

1 medium shallot, diced
    (⅛-inch pieces)

½ cup extra virgin olive oil

¼ cup fresh lemon juice
    (from 1 to 2 medium lemons)

cracked black pepper

Beets are one of those vegetables that I sometimes forget how much I love. When they're in season, they can be just as sweet as candy, while retaining a hint of that earthiness of the best root vegetables. In Nantucket, we get lovely local beets from late summer into fall, so I associate them with warm-weather times. (Fortunately, though, you can find good ones year-round in most markets.) Adding a fresh mint dressing complements the beets' flavors and makes for a refreshing first course or, even better, lively side dish for fish or meat dishes on a warm summer day.

1. Preheat the oven to 400°F.

2. Place the beets in a large ovenproof glass casserole and cover with the salt. Bake for about 1 hour, or until fork tender.

3. Place the beets in a stainless-steel bowl to cool: Use a towel to wipe off the excess salt. Peel the beets, cut them into 1-inch cubes, and place them in a clean stainless-steel bowl. Add the mint, shallots, olive oil, and lemon juice. Season with pepper (bearing in mind the beets will already be salty from the baking process), toss thoroughly, and serve.

CHICKEN AL MATTONE WITH BROCCOLI RABE AND LEMON RISOTTO

SERVES 4 TO 6

One 2½- to 3-pound chicken, cut in half and partially deboned

4 tablespoons grapeseed oil

2 lemons, cut in half

2 fresh rosemary sprigs

4 garlic cloves

1 teaspoon kosher salt

½ teaspoon cracked black pepper

pinch of red pepper flakes

chopped fresh Italian (flat-leaf) parsley for garnish

2 regular masonry bricks, wrapped in aluminum foil

Lemon Risotto (page 38)

Broccoli Rabe (page 39)

Many people believe ordering chicken out is the ultimate litmus test: If a place can't do right by chicken, what can it do? Since my restaurants were all about family-style dining, we had to offer at least one outstanding chicken dish. This one quickly became a signature. Its main attractions are simple seasonings—garlic, lemon, and a hint of hot red pepper—and meat that's seared and crispy on the outside, moist and delectable inside. This dish was inspired by the summer I spent cooking in Umbria, where I learned a lot about grilled meats. Legend has it that the masons who laid the cobblestones of Rome would build small roadside fires and grill chickens under bricks for a quick, delicious lunch. (*Mattone*, of course, is Italian for "brick.") This is my home version, done in a sauté pan and finished in the oven, to bring out the natural flavor of the chicken, as opposed to the flavor of the grill.

INGREDIENT NOTES: Ask for a halved, partially deboned chicken, meaning the ribs and other small bones around the cavity are taken out but the drumstick, thigh, and wing bones are left in for easy handling. Any butcher will know what this means. If you don't have any loose bricks around, you may want to pick up a couple at a building supply or gardening center. (As an alternative, use a cast-iron pan.) You can reuse the bricks and apply the technique to pork, steak, or even fish, though chicken remains the classic.

TIMING NOTES: The chicken is marinated overnight in the refrigerator in advance. Before cooking, have your ingredients for all three recipes prepped and ready; once you put the chicken in the oven, make the risotto. The broccoli rabe can be blanched in advance, set aside, and finished in a few minutes just prior to serving.

1. Place the chicken halves, 2 tablespoons of the grapeseed oil, the juice of 1 lemon, the rosemary sprigs, and garlic cloves in a glass or ceramic shallow dish and mix to combine. Cover and place in the refrigerator to marinate overnight.

2. Preheat the oven to 400°F. Set up the racks for 2 sauté pans.

3. Put 1 tablespoon of the remaining grapeseed oil in each of two large oven-safe sauté pans over high heat. When the oil has reached smoke point, place the chicken halves in the pans, skin side down, and season with the salt and pepper. Reduce the heat to medium and sear until the skin is golden brown, 4 to 5 minutes.

4. Place one brick on top of each chicken half (still skin side down). Place both pans, with the chicken halves and bricks, in the oven to roast for 20 minutes. When pressed lightly, the chicken juices should run clear, with no blood.

5. Transfer the chicken halves, skin side up, to a serving plate. Squeeze over the juice from the 2 remaining lemon halves, sprinkle with the red pepper flakes, garnish with the chopped parsley, and serve.

Lemon Risotto

2 tablespoons grapeseed oil

1 cup coarsely chopped onions
(from about 1 medium onion)

2 cups Carnaroli rice

½ cup fresh lemon juice (from
about 3 lemons)

½ cup limoncello

6 cups water, room temperature

½ teaspoon kosher salt

¼ teaspoon cracked black
pepper

2 tablespoons unsalted butter

½ cup grated Parmigiano-
Reggiano, plus more
for garnish

1 heaping tablespoon finely
chopped fresh Italian
(flat-leaf) parsley

This is one of my favorite risotto recipes. I think of the lemon flavoring as a very Sicilian touch. It's relatively light for a risotto, and I think it provides a nice complement to the lemon flavor in the chicken. You can buy the limoncello or make it yourself.

1. Put the grapeseed oil and onions in a 3-quart saucepan at room temperature. Place the saucepan over medium heat and sauté the onions, stirring occasionally with a wooden spoon, until translucent, 3 to 4 minutes. The onions should not take on any color; lower the heat if necessary.

2. Stir the rice into the onions in the pan and toast it for 1 to 2 minutes, until it dries out and the kernels become opaque. While toasting, agitate the pan occasionally to keep the rice from sticking to the bottom. Add the lemon juice and the limoncello and let evaporate. Begin to add the water 2 cups at a time, continuing to stir the rice as it releases its starch. (The water will be added in three stages.) Continue to agitate the pan occasionally to prevent sticking. Drag the spoon through the rice and when the rice is thick enough to reveal a pathway, add the next 2 cups water and repeat the procedure.

3. After adding the final 2 cups water, stir in the salt, pepper, butter, and grated Parmigiano-Reggiano. Serve immediately with a sprinkling of parsley and extra cheese.

NOTE: When the risotto is done, it should have a silky appearance. The individual kernels should still be discreet and visible. The texture of a risotto should be very creamy, but the grains themselves should be toothsome; they should retain some bite. You should be able to taste the featured flavor(s)—in this case a subtle hint of lemon—not just the starchiness of the rice.

Broccoli Rabe

2 tablespoons plus 1 teaspoon
　 kosher salt

2 pounds broccoli rabe, washed
　 and trimmed

2 tablespoons grapeseed oil

1 garlic clove, sliced

pinch of red pepper flakes

juice of one lemon

¼ teaspoon cracked black
　 pepper

1. Fill a 5-quart stockpot half full of water, add 2 tablespoons of the salt, and bring to a boil over high heat. Prepare an ice bath. Blanch the broccoli rabe by dropping it into the pot of boiling water for 30 seconds. Remove the broccoli rabe from the pot, plunge it into the ice bath, then transfer to a colander and drain.

2. Place the grapeseed oil and garlic in a 10-inch skillet over medium heat. Lightly sauté for 1 minute, making sure it does not color or burn (lower the heat and/or remove the pan from the burner if necessary). Add the blanched, drained broccoli rabe to the pan and lightly toss to cook evenly, 2 to 3 minutes. Add the red pepper flakes, lemon juice, the remaining 1 teaspoon salt, and the pepper, and serve.

HOMESPUN GOAT MILK GELATO

SERVES 6 TO 8

5 cups fresh goat milk

1 vanilla bean, scraped (save the pod to flavor a jar of sugar)

10 large egg yolks

1½ cups sugar

½ teaspoon kosher salt

When Colleen was developing the dessert menu for our first restaurant, she went in search of the best fresh local milk for making gelato. She stumbled upon a local farmer who asked if she would be interested in goat milk. Why not? It worked out well, and Colleen successfully experimented with a number of flavors; this is the basic recipe. Goat milk is lactose free, making it easier to digest, and has less fat than cow's milk, so it yields a lighter ice cream. If you can get some fresh goat milk right off the farm, great; if not, the good news is quality goat milk has become a lot easier to find in grocery stores.

1. Place the milk and vanilla bean in a medium heavy-bottomed saucepan over low to medium heat until warm.

2. Place the egg yolks, sugar, and salt in a stainless-steel bowl and beat with a whisk until the mixture is a pale yellowish white. Temper the warm milk into the yolk mixture by carefully whisking about 1 cup of the milk into the yolks. Then, after they are well incorporated, whisk the entire yolk mixture back into the remainder of the warm milk. Cook over low heat, stirring continuously for about 8 minutes, until the gelato mixture has thickened slightly and coats the back of a spoon.

3. Prepare an ice bath: Place a stainless-steel bowl over another, slightly larger bowl filled with ice water. Pass the gelato mixture through a fine-mesh strainer into the top bowl. Remove the vanilla bean, then place the mixture in an ice cream machine and process according to the manufacturer's instructions. Serve.

~2~

· HAVING · COMPANY

Everyday Dinners for Family and Guests

{SERVING 6 TO 8}

OVERLEAF: Branzino in Porchetta (page 64).

Little Nonna's Table

My grandmother little nonna's expandable table defines the occasions for this chapter. The golden wheat color of its enamel top holds a special place in my childhood memories. As a very young boy, I would go over to my grandmother's apartment after school and she would often whip up my favorite snack—creamed corn with crushed *friselle* (the inspiration behind my recipe on page 124 of chapter 5.) My grandmother's table was normally pushed into the corner of her small apartment kitchen. When she had company, she would move it to the center of the room and pull out the flaps to easily accommodate all of us. Little Nonna's table has a drawer in the middle of one side that always held her silverware. In the back of that drawer there's a separate compartment that I made into my own special hiding place for personal items like my candies, Matchbox cars, and Super Balls.

When the time came for my grandmother to settle my great-grandmother's estate, I made sure we saved a few key items, including both Big Nonna's and Little Nonna's tables, Big Nonna's kitchen sink, and the mason jars they used for putting away tomatoes and other vegetables. Although I was just entering culinary school at the time, I knew I wanted to preserve those traditions and re-create the ambiance of their kitchens some day. Like Formica countertops and antique Frigidaire refrigerators, Little Nonna's old enamel table evokes a certain era—the 1940s and 1950s, when family-style dining became less formal and often moved to the casual comfort of the kitchen. It is both a timeless classic and a one-of-kind heirloom I feel lucky to have inherited.

Having company doesn't need to be a huge undertaking. One of the main reasons I fell in love with Italian culture was its ease at welcoming and accommodating guests. In this chapter, you'll discover streamlined ways to impress company without taking up too much time in preparation. The scenario is a weekday meal serving six to eight people, starting with the nuclear family and including other family members, friends, and neighbors. The recipes are designed for easy entertaining. Most of them add a sophisticated touch that will have your guests craving more—and perhaps even asking for a copy of the recipe.

This chapter features several preparations truly representative not only of Italian-style family dining but of my family in particular. This starts with the *pizza rustica*, a multigenerational recipe that was ever-present at holiday celebrations and was passed down from my great-grandmother to my grandmother to my mother. You'll also find my grandmother's recipe for stuffed artichokes; a salad—the Iceberg wedges with Gorgonzola dressing inspired by my mother—and a clever side dish invented by my older daughter, Vivian (Baby Carrots with Almond Pesto).

MARINATED IMPORTED OLIVES

SERVES 6 TO 8

6 cups olives, pits left in
   (3 cups black Cerignola,
   3 cups green Cerignola, or
   another combination of your
   choice; see ingredient note)

1 tablespoon fennel pollen

2 tablespoons ¼-inch strips
   lemon zest

1 teaspoon red pepper flakes

½ cup extra virgin olive oil

About a quarter of the olives grown in the entire world come from Italy, and there are literally hundreds of local varieties found all over the peninsula. The best-known are Ligurian, Ponentine, Cerignola, and Gaeta, from the towns of the same names on the coast not far from Naples. There are also many types grown in Tuscany, Le Marche, throughout the south, and in Sicily. The more southern varieties tend to be larger and milder in flavor, while the northern ones are smaller and more potent. Cerignola, which are called for in this recipe, originally come from Puglia and are large, light green-colored, and fleshy. Black olives—whatever the variety—are the ones that have been left to ripen on the trees. Tuscan olives are always harvested green because of the potential for frost damage if they are left to ripen fully.

For my marinade, I like to use fennel pollen, which comes from the wild fennel plants that grow roadside throughout Italy. The pollen, which I first came across in Umbria, has the aniselike flavor of fennel bulbs or seeds but it's subtler, more floral. It's also a bit sweet so I call for some peperoncini (hot red pepper flakes) to add kick and provide balance. I almost always serve these olives with an antipasto spread; they work well with both white and red wines and complement many other appetizer dishes. You can use this same marinade recipe for lamb, chicken, or fish.

INGREDIENT NOTE: Be sure to buy olives that have been simply brine-cured (not prepared with olive oil or other ingredients), so you can create your own marinade for them to soak up. Substitute any type of olives you like, including French picholines, Greek kalamatas, or Spanish manzanillas.

PLACE THE OLIVES in a stainless-steel bowl. Add the fennel pollen, lemon zest, red pepper flakes, and olive oil. Toss thoroughly until well mixed, then place in a non-reactive container, sealed or covered with plastic wrap. Place in the refrigerator to marinate for 24 hours. Remove from the refrigerator 30 minutes before serving.

STORAGE: The olives can be stored, tightly covered, in the refrigerator for up to 30 days.

PIZZA RUSTICA

MAKES 2 PIZZAS, 13 X 9 INCHES EACH

FOR THE CRUST

5 cups all-purpose flour, plus more for flouring

2 teaspoons kosher salt

2 teaspoons cracked black pepper

4 large brown eggs

½ cup cold water

4½ tablespoons extra virgin olive oil, plus more for oiling

FOR THE FILLING

2 dozen large brown eggs

1 pound boiled ham (prosciutto cotto), cut into 1-inch cubes

1 pound imported prosciutto, cut into 1-inch cubes

½ pound Genoa salami, cut into 1-inch cubes

3 cups grated pecorino Romano

1 pound whole milk ricotta

2 teaspoons cracked black pepper

I doubt there is an Italian or Italian-American family that doesn't have at least one version of a traditional *pizza rustica* recipe they dust off for a special occasion. I grew up with several variations of these savory pies, served as part of the antipasto course for Christmas and Easter. My great-grandmother made her *pizza rustica* with salami, prosciutto, and ham. My grandmother followed the same recipe, except she used only pepperoni. My mother took up my grandmother's recipe and we called it "pepperoni pie." Here I'm reverting to Big Nonna's recipe. In any case, if it's Christmas or Easter in one of our households, you know somebody is baking a *pizza rustica* that will make everybody happy. It's rich, filling, delicious, and very hard to put down. Beware of overeating! (I know from experience.)

INGREDIENT NOTE: Buy the prosciutto and ham in chunks at least 1 inch thick (not thin slices) so they can be cut into cubes.

TIMING NOTE: The pies require 2 hours of baking time.

1. First prepare the dough for the crust: Place the flour, salt, pepper, eggs, water, and olive oil in the bowl of an electric mixer with the paddle attachment. Beat on medium speed until thoroughly mixed, 6 to 8 minutes.

2. Remove the dough from the mixer, place it on a well-floured work surface, and knead by hand until smooth and malleable, 8 to 10 minutes. Place the dough in a lightly oiled stainless-steel or ceramic bowl, cover with a kitchen towel, and set aside at room temperature for 10 minutes.

3. Meanwhile, preheat the oven to 325°F and lightly oil two 13 x 9-inch baking pans.

4. Cut the dough into four equal portions and roll each out to a 12 x 8-inch rectangle about ⅛ inch thick. Transfer one dough to each of the prepared baking pans.

5. To make the filling, place 10 of the eggs in a large stainless-steel bowl and beat well. Add the ham, prosciutto, salami, pecorino Romano, ricotta, and pepper and mix until thoroughly combined. Divide the filling into two equal portions and spread each one evenly on top of the dough in the baking pans. Place one of the remaining pieces of dough on top of the filling in each pan, pinching the edges of the dough together and then securing them by pinching the edges to the rims of the pans.

6. Beat the remaining 2 eggs and brush the top of each pie with the egg wash until well coated. Place each pan on top of a baking sheet and bake for 2 hours. Remove from the oven, let the pies cool to room temperature, cut into wedges, and serve.

STORAGE: The pizzas can be stored in the fridge, wrapped well in plastic or in an airtight container, for up to 2 weeks. Let come to room temperature before serving.

CHICKEN LIVER CROSTINI

SERVES 6 TO 8 (18 TO 20 CROSTINI)

½ pound chicken livers

1 heaping tablespoon capers

2 tablespoons grapeseed oil

½ medium Spanish onion, sliced ¼ inch thick

3 fresh sage sprigs

1 anchovy fillet

pinch of red pepper flakes

½ cup vin santo

2 cups heavy cream

1 baguette, sliced ¼-thick on a bias, to make ovals

kosher salt and cracked black pepper

I discovered the authentic Florentine version of this recipe while working at Il Cibrèo in Florence, and brought it back to make my own adaptation a signature dish at my restaurants in New York and Nantucket. Crostini are little toasted rounds of bread with a brushing of olive oil that are most often graced with a savory topping. Spread with a chicken liver puree, they are considered *the* quintessential Tuscan antipasto. They can stand alone or be a highlight of an assorted platter along with cured meats, olives, raw fennel, white beans, pickled mushrooms, and so forth. I added a few twists to the basic Tuscan recipe, including the heavy cream for richness and the capers and vin santo, which provide a balance of sweet, salty and nutty flavor accents. I also serve the toasts on the side so people can spread as much (or as little) of the liver puree as they like.

INGREDIENT NOTE: For the *crostini*, you want small oval-shaped slices of bread, so a baguette works best. Almost any type of high-quality, baguette-style white bread works. I don't recommend a multigrain bread because it brings too much of its own flavor to the equation.

1. Preheat the oven to 400°F. Rinse, drain, and lay the chicken livers out on paper towels to dry. Rinse the capers under cold running water and drain.

2. Heat the grapeseed oil in a large 10-inch sauté pan over medium-high heat. Add the onions, lower the heat to medium-low, and cook until translucent, 8 to 10 minutes, stirring frequently to avoid sticking.

3. Add the chicken livers, capers, sage, anchovy, and red pepper flakes, and continue cooking over medium heat, stirring occasionally, until the livers are lightly browned, 8 to 10 minutes. Deglaze the pan with the vin santo, then add the heavy cream and continue cooking over medium heat for 5 to 7 minutes more, again stirring frequently, until the cream is reduced by about half.

4. Place the slices of baguette on a baking sheet and toast in the oven until lightly golden in color, 6 to 8 minutes.

5. Working in batches if necessary, transfer the chicken liver mixture (while still warm) from the pan into the bowl of a food processor with the blade attachment and puree for 2 to 4 minutes. Once pureed, season with salt and pepper and set aside to come to room temperature. Serve with the crostini on the side.

STORAGE: The puree can be stored in a ceramic or glass bowl in the refrigerator for up to 2 weeks, covered snugly with plastic wrap. The wrap should be laid directly on the puree, with no air in between, to avoid oxidation of its surface.

OCTOPUS SALAD WITH SHAVED CELERY, PICKLED RED ONION, AND PINE NUTS

SERVES 6 TO 8

3 pounds baby octopus, cleaned
and left whole

2 cups dry white wine

1 medium Spanish onion, sliced
½ inch thick (about 2 cups)

1 bay leaf

3 celery stalks

1 large red onion, thinly sliced

1 cup red wine vinegar

½ cup pine nuts, toasted

½ cup extra virgin olive oil

kosher salt and cracked black
pepper

Octopus is an acquired taste, and I think this salad combination is a great way to introduce it to newcomers, as I was on a birthday trip to the Ligurian coast in November 1995. Octopus has a strong flavor and can be chewy in texture. The crunchy, watery celery helps moderate it, as do the vinegary pickled onions. There is a fine line between undercooking and overcooking octopus. First, it's important to start octopus in a pot of water at room temperature and gradually bring the water to a boil rather than plunge it into an already-boiling pot, which can make it tough. Test the octopus to make sure it's fork tender to your satisfaction. A fork should go in quite easily; the octopus shouldn't be rubbery or resistant. In addition, if you like, put a cork in the cooking water to help tenderize the octopus. It's an old Spanish myth I learned from a fellow chef, Diego, when I worked at Il Buco in Manhattan. As I recall, his family roots were in Gaeta, Italy, but he grew up by the sea in Spain.

INGREDIENT NOTE: There are a few online sources where you can find fresh, refrigerated, and/or flash-frozen octopus; generally speaking, your best bet is to check your local Asian and Italian seafood markets. Usually, the octopus you find will be of the smaller or "baby" size, which is what we call for here.

1. Place the octopus, white wine, onions, and bay leaf in a 5-quart saucepan. Add enough water to cover and bring to a boil over medium-high heat. Lower the heat to medium-low and simmer until the octopus is fork tender, 45 minutes to 1 hour.

2. Prepare an ice bath: Fill a large bowl with water and ice, leaving enough room for the celery. Use a vegetable peeler to strip off the outer skin of the celery, then, with a sharp knife, slice the celery on the bias into strips about 2 inches long and ⅛ inch thick. Place the celery strips in the ice bath for about 45 minutes; they will take on a curly shape.

3. Place the red onions in a 2-quart saucepan with the red wine vinegar and 2 cups of water. Bring to a boil over medium heat, lower the heat, and simmer for 20 minutes. Remove the pan from the heat and let cool for 10 minutes. Drain the onions and set aside.

4. Drain the contents of the octopus pot, discard the onion and bay leaf, and set the octopus aside to cool. Chop the octopus into 1-inch pieces and place in a large stainless-steel bowl. Drain the shaved celery and add it to the bowl with the octopus. Add the pickled red onions, toasted pine nuts, and olive oil and toss well. Season with salt and pepper, transfer to a serving bowl, and serve.

CLASSIC RIBOLLITA

SERVES 6 TO 8

1 medium (leftover or stale) loaf Italian bread

1 cup diced Spanish onions, (¼-inch cubes; from ½ medium onion)

1 cup diced carrots (¼-inch cubes; from 1 medium carrot)

1 cup diced celery (¼-inch cubes; from 1 large stalk)

1 cup diced leeks, white and light green parts only (¼-inch cubes; from 1 large leek)

2 cups chopped savoy cabbage (½-inch pieces; from ½ medium head)

2 cups chopped Tuscan or black kale (½-inch pieces; from ½ bunch, see Ingredient Note, page 22)

6 cups vegetable stock

kosher salt and cracked black pepper

6 to 8 tablespoons extra virgin olive oil

This is a traditional Tuscan soup I first learned about from Chef Fabio Picchi of Il Cibrèo. He used to call it the "garbage pot of soups," because it includes not only a lot of leftover vegetables but stale bread as its key ingredients. *Ribollita*, which means "reboiled," is among the most famous of the classic Tuscan peasant dishes. In its simplest incarnation, it is nothing more than reheated minestrone with leftover bread added to make a hearty meal of it. Crucial to the cooking process here is the long, slow simmering, which causes the stale bread to melt and all the wonderful garden vegetable flavors to meld perfectly.

INGREDIENT NOTE: The best bread for this recipe is any type of day-old (or older) rustic Italian bread; I highly recommend toasting it as a flavor boost. There's no concern about its getting too hard because the simmering will break it down completely. For the cabbage, I always use savoy; it has the finest flavor and consistency.

1. Preheat the oven to 400°F.

2. Break the bread into 3-inch chunks, lay them on a baking sheet, and toast in the oven until golden in color, about 10 minutes.

3. Place the onions, carrots, celery, leeks, cabbage, kale, and vegetable stock in a large 5-quart stockpot over medium-high heat and bring to a boil. Lower the heat to maintain a simmer and add the toasted bread, making sure it is completely submerged. Stir often so the soup does not stick to the bottom of the pot or burn. Continue to simmer for about 1 hour. The soup should attain a thick glossy consistency as the bread melts.

4. Pass the soup through a food mill into a serving container large enough to hold the entire amount (alternatively, use a stand or immersion blender). Season with salt and pepper. Ladle the soup into bowls, garnish each bowl with a drizzle of extra virgin olive oil, and serve warm (but not piping hot).

BRINED PORK LOIN WITH CARAMELIZED
SALSIFY AND TURNIPS

SERVES 6 TO 8

FOR THE BRINE

4 quarts water

¾ cup kosher salt

1 bay leaf

½ cup black peppercorns

---

one 6-pound boneless pork loin, trimmed

2 teaspoons kosher salt, plus more to taste

1 teaspoon cracked black pepper, plus more to taste

2 tablespoons grapeseed oil

1 medium Spanish onion, cut into 1-inch cubes

5 cups peeled, chopped salsify (1-inch pieces; from about 8 pieces)

5 cups peeled, chopped white turnip (1-inch cubes; from about 3 turnips)

1 fresh rosemary sprig

extra virgin olive oil for drizzling, optional

Brining has long been the professional chef's secret method for keeping some of the leaner cuts of meat tender and moist. Soaking or marinating meat in a salt solution tenderizes it and adds water, which in turn slowly cooks out when it's in the oven. Since roasting is one of the more dehydrating forms of cooking, adding extra moisture is a good guarantee your meat won't dry out. Brining has become increasingly popular with home cooks, as has the practice of adding flavor by introducing more ingredients than just salt to the brine. I find brining works great with pork loin, which is pleasantly mild, and in this simple recipe I add a bay leaf and peppercorns for a subtle flavor accent.

INGREDIENT NOTE: Salsify is a root vegetable similar in appearance to a parsnip, usually with a grayish or yellowish skin. The black-skinned variety is called *scorzonera* in Italy. It has a slightly bitter, earthy taste that I find works very nicely in combination with turnips, which develop some sweetness when cooked. Salsify may not be the most common item in the vegetable section of your local grocery, but I recommend going a bit out of the way to find it. You will be pleasantly surprised when you caramelize it alongside the turnips. Salsify season is late fall and early winter. In a pinch, parsnips can be substituted.

TIMING NOTE: The pork loin needs to be refrigerated in the brine for 24 hours.

1. First brine the pork loin: Place the water, salt, bay leaf, and peppercorns in a large 5-quart saucepan over medium heat. Bring to a boil and cook for 6 to 8 minutes. Remove from the heat and set aside to cool. Once the brine has cooled to room temperature, add the pork loin, cover the pan, and place it in the refrigerator for 24 hours. Transfer the pork loin to a rack inside a roasting pan and let sit at room temperature for 20 minutes before roasting.

2. Preheat the oven to 400°F.

3. Season the meat all over with the salt and pepper. Roast for about 45 minutes, until the juices run clear when pierced with the tip of a sharp knife, or the meat measures 145–150°F on a meat thermometer. Remove the roast loin from the oven, tent with aluminum foil, and let rest for 20 minutes.

4. Place the grapeseed oil in a large 12-inch sauté pan over medium heat. Add the onions, salsify, turnips, and rosemary and cook, stirring often, until the vegetables are deep golden in color and nicely caramelized, 10 to 12 minutes. Season with salt and pepper, and arrange on a serving platter.

5. Cut the pork loin into 1-inch-thick slices and place on top of the vegetables. Drizzle with extra virgin olive oil, if desired.

ICEBERG WEDGES WITH CREAMY GORGONZOLA DRESSING AND BREAD CRUMBS

SERVES 6 TO 8

1 large head iceberg lettuce

1 pound Gorgonzola dolce

1 medium shallot

½ cup extra virgin olive oil

2 tablespoons cider vinegar

3 fresh thyme sprigs, leaves only

1 cup heavy cream

kosher salt and cracked black pepper

¾ cup unseasoned bread crumbs, toasted

My mom often served one of the great American salads, iceberg lettuce with a creamy blue cheese dressing. This is my Italianized version of that nostalgic classic, featuring Gorgonzola, of which there are two types: the *piccante* ("spicy," which is longer aged, drier, and stronger) and *dolce* ("sweet," which is younger, milder, and creamier). Whatever kind of blue cheese you use for the original "American" version of this salad, I defy you to pick a cheese more delicious than a genuine top-quality Gorgonzola dolce. The best Stilton may come close, but I'm convinced there's none better than the Gorgonzola.

1. Remove and discard the tough outer leaves of the lettuce. Slice the head vertically, from the root to the top, into 6 or 8 equal-size wedges (about 2 inches thick at their outer edge).

2. Place the Gorgonzola, shallot, olive oil, vinegar, thyme, and heavy cream in a blender and blend on medium-high speed until the dressing achieves a creamy consistency, 3 to 5 minutes. Season with salt and pepper.

3. Place a wedge of iceberg lettuce on each plate. Pour an equal portion of dressing on each wedge, garnish with toasted bread crumbs, and serve.

BABY CARROTS WITH ALMOND PESTO

SERVES 6 TO 8

FOR THE PESTO

2 cups almonds, shells and
   husks removed, toasted

1 garlic clove

¾ cup extra virgin olive oil

kosher salt and cracked black
   pepper

---

4 tablespoons unsalted butter

3 pounds baby carrots, blanched

cracked black pepper

I've been lucky with my kids: Because they've grown up in and around our family and restaurant kitchens, I've never had to bother them about what to eat. Once my older daughter, Vivian, learned a few basics, I encouraged her to try cooking on her own. It turns out she loves to experiment with different combinations of ingredients. I taught her how to make pesto, and she came up with this almond variation. Baby carrots are one of the principal foods parents use to coax their kids toward healthier eating: they're cute, sweet tasting, and bite size. This is Vivian's recipe for them, giving her and her siblings no excuse for not eating their vegetables and adding a really nice side dish to the family dining repertoire.

1. First make the pesto: Place the almonds, garlic, and olive oil in a blender and blend at high speed for 2 to 3 minutes. Season with salt and pepper.

2. Place the butter in a large 12-inch skillet over medium heat. Add the carrots and sauté, stirring or tossing occasionally, for 3 to 5 minutes. Transfer the carrots and butter to a serving dish or platter, add the almond pesto on top, and serve.

STORAGE: If there is leftover pesto or you make extra, it can be stored in the refrigerator for up to 2 weeks, in an airtight glass container, with a thin layer of olive oil on top to protect it.

SPICY CHICKPEA SOUP WITH LAMB POLPETTINE AND CRÈME FRAICHE

SERVES 6 TO 8

FOR THE CRÈME FRAÎCHE

2 tablespoons buttermilk

2 cups heavy cream, warm

2 pounds (4 cups) dried chickpeas

1 medium carrot

1 medium Spanish onion

2 medium celery stalks

2 tablespoons grapeseed oil,
    plus more for oiling

1 garlic clove, thinly sliced

½ teaspoon red pepper flakes

1 fresh rosemary sprig

zest of 1 lemon

4 quarts chicken broth

It's easy to detect the influences of northern Africa in many aspects of southern Italian cuisine, particularly in Sicily. They are evident in this recipe, which uses lamb for the *polpettine* ("meatballs") and adds them to spicy chickpea soup. While chickpeas (*ceci* in Italy) are most associated with the Middle East, they are also featured in a few excellent traditional Italian dishes—soups like this one, but also with pasta and in salads. This recipe is reminiscent of the so-called Italian Wedding Soup, the term my parents' and grandparents' generations used for a *minestra maritata*, an old Neapolitan favorite combining vegetables and meat (either sausage or meatballs) in broth. It's not that the soup was served at weddings, but rather the name originates from the soup's successful marriage of meat and vegetables.

INGREDIENT NOTE: Here, I'm calling for two ingredients that will develop into crème fraiche overnight but, if it's available at your market already made, buy it and skip this step. I prefer to buy dried chickpeas and apply one of the soaking procedures. If you want to avoid preliminary steps altogether, good-quality canned or precooked chickpeas can be substituted, but I've found that dried chickpeas have better flavor and texture.

TIMING NOTE: The crème fraiche develops overnight in advance, and can be stored for up to 2 weeks in an airtight container in the refrigerator. The chickpeas can be soaked overnight in advance or you can use the "quick soak" procedure in step 2.

1. First prepare the crème fraîche: Place the buttermilk and heavy cream in a stainless-steel bowl, cover with plastic wrap, and set aside in a cool place for 24 hours.

2. Place the chickpeas in a saucepot large enough to hold the entire quantity plus enough water to cover by 2 inches. Add the water, bring to a boil over high heat, and cook for 3 to 4 minutes. Cover the pot, remove it from the heat, and set aside for 1 hour. When ready to cook, drain the chickpeas. Skip this step if soaking chickpeas overnight or using canned or precooked chickpeas.

3. Preheat the oven to 400°F.

4. Place the carrot, onion, and celery in the bowl of a food processor with the blade attachment and process until all they are finely chopped.

5. Place the grapeseed oil in a large 5-quart saucepan over medium heat. Add the chopped vegetables and cook, stirring occasionally, until the onions are translucent, 3 to 4 minutes. Add the garlic, red pepper flakes, rosemary, lemon zest, and chickpeas, and stir well to combine. Add the chicken broth, raise the heat and bring to a boil. Lower the heat to maintain a simmer and cook until the chickpeas are soft, 45 minutes to 1 hour. Working in batches, puree the chickpea soup in a blender at medium speed for 3 to 4 minutes.

Polpettine

2 pounds ground lamb

1 garlic clove, minced

½ cup finely chopped fresh
    Italian (flat-leaf) parsley

1 teaspoon sweet paprika

¼ teaspoon red pepper flakes

1 large brown egg

2 teaspoons kosher salt, plus
    more to taste

1 teaspoon cracked black
    pepper, plus more to taste

1. Place the lamb, garlic, parsley, paprika, red pepper flakes, and egg in a large stainless-steel bowl. Season with the salt and pepper and mix by hand, using your fingers to thoroughly combine all the ingredients. In the palms of your hands, roll about 2 tablespoons of the mixture at a time into meatballs about 1 inch in diameter. Place the meatballs close together (so they are just touching) on a lightly oiled baking sheet and bake for about 15 minutes, or until cooked through. Remove from the oven and set aside to cool.

2. Place the pureed soup in a large 5-quart saucepan over medium heat and bring to a boil. Add the meatballs, lower the heat, and simmer for about 20 minutes. Season with salt and pepper. Ladle equal portions of soup and meatballs into bowls, garnish each with a dollop of crème fraîche, and serve hot.

CIDER-BRAISED CABBAGE WITH PANCETTA

SERVES 6 TO 8

2 tablespoons grapeseed oil

½ pound pancetta, diced
(¼-inch cubes)

1 medium Spanish onion, thinly
sliced

1 large savoy cabbage, split in
half and sliced ½ inch thick

1 cup cider vinegar

kosher salt and cracked black
pepper

Cabbage was a staple of meals with my father's Hungarian-Polish side of the family. Braising the cabbage in cider vinegar and onions was standard procedure in those households. All kinds of pork products, such as bacon, were also quite common. In keeping with my passion for Italianizing my world of food, this version includes pancetta. This is a quick, easy-to-prepare side dish that goes great alongside a main course of fish.

INGREDIENT NOTE: Bacon and *pancetta* are both prepared from pork bellies, and pancetta is often referred to as "the Italian version of bacon." Generally speaking, the difference is that bacon is brined then smoked, whereas pancetta is salt-cured and may be seasoned with pepper and other spices. *Pancetta* has a sweeter, more refined flavor; bacon is stronger and, of course, smoky. Bacon is usually presented in slabs that are sliced a bit thicker than *pancetta*, which is sliced thin from the rolled-up cured bellies.

PLACE THE GRAPESEED oil in a 10-inch skillet over medium heat. Add the pancetta and cook, stirring regularly, until golden brown and crispy, 5 to 6 minutes. Add the onions and continue cooking until translucent, 3 to 4 minutes more. Add the cabbage and cook, stirring occasionally, until all the leaves have wilted, 3 to 4 minutes. Add the vinegar, cover the pan, and cook for 6 to 8 minutes more. Remove the lid, season with salt and pepper, and serve.

BRANZINO IN PORCHETTA

SERVES 6 TO 8

1 medium carrot, cut into 1-inch
    pieces

1 medium Spanish onion, cut
    into 1-inch pieces

2 medium celery stalks, cut into
    1-inch pieces

2 fresh thyme sprigs, leaves only

2 pounds pork fatback, cut
    into 1-inch cubes, at room
    temperature

3 large whole branzini (2 pounds
    each), gutted and scaled

2 teaspoons kosher salt

1 teaspoon cracked black
    pepper

2 tablespoons grapeseed oil

½ cup finely chopped fresh
    Italian (flat-leaf) parsley

In porchetta is a way of using pork fat to marinate other meats for roasting, ensuring that they stay moist and adding a unique extra dimension of flavor. I learned this method during my time in central Umbria. I worked the entire summer of 1999 at an *agriturismo* in Bevagna, near Todi, across the valley from Assisi, before returning to open my restaurant in Nantucket the following summer. I suppose it's ironic that I got the inspiration for several of my best signature fish dishes while cooking in one of the few landlocked regions of Italy. There they used trout from the Lago di Trasimeno, by far the largest lake south of the river Po.

In porchetta can be applied to chicken and turkey, as well as to whole fish (as it is used here). Use the same pork fat–and-vegetable stuffing, but simply rub the cavities with it and then slip portions of it between the skin and the flesh.

INGREDIENT NOTES: Branzino is a European sea bass, found in the sea and saltwater lakes. Orata, trout, or another medium-size, white-fleshed fish, such as red snapper, can be substituted. Fatback is pure unsalted, uncured pork fat used to make lard and cracklings. Lard can be substituted.

TIMING NOTE: The stuffed, rubbed fish needs to marinate for 6 to 8 hours in the refrigerator.

1. Place the carrots, onions, and celery in the bowl of a food processor with the blade attachment. Add the thyme and process on medium speed for 2 to 3 minutes, until finely chopped. Add the fatback and process for 3 to 4 more minutes, until the mixture attains a creamy consistency.

2. Season the fish inside and out with the salt and pepper. Stuff the fish cavities with half the vegetable-fat mixture; they should be full but loosely packed. Rub the remaining half of the filling all over the outside of the fish, making sure some of it is pushed into the gills. Wrap the fish in plastic, lay it on a large baking sheet, and marinate it in the refrigerator for 6 to 8 hours. Remove the fish from the fridge 20 minutes before cooking.

3. Preheat the oven to 400°F.

4. Place the grapeseed oil in a large 12-inch skillet over medium heat. Brown the fish, one at a time, 3 to 4 minutes on each side. Transfer the fish, side by side, to a baking pan, drizzling the fat from the skillet on top. Bake the fish in the oven for 8 to 10 minutes, until the flesh easily flakes away from the bone when just pierced with a fork. Transfer the fish, side by side, to a large serving platter. Use a large knife or spatula to carefully lift the meat from the bones, divide the fillets into equal portions, garnish with the parsley, and serve.

NONNA'S STUFFED ARTICHOKES

SERVES 6 TO 8

4 cups fresh bread crumbs

1 cup grated pecorino Romano cheese

1 cup finely chopped fresh Italian (flat-leaf) parsley

5 garlic cloves, finely minced

½ cup extra virgin olive oil

8 medium artichokes

Here is a recipe that brings back vivid and fond childhood memories. Come family dinners or parties, my Big Nonna would always make her stuffed artichokes, served as an appetizer throughout their winter season. I remember it as a special treat, making me feel like a real grown-up, to have a whole artichoke to myself and to take pleasure in meticulously scraping all the flesh off the leaves right down to the heart. In Italy, artichokes are thought of as the quintessential Roman vegetable, but of course that doesn't mean they aren't served with pride throughout the peninsula. Their subtle flavor, as mild as it is, not only stands up to, but is wonderfully enhanced by, the assertive combination of garlic, pecorino, and extra virgin olive oil.

1. Preheat the oven to 400°F.

2. Place the bread crumbs, pecorino Romano, parsley, garlic, and olive oil in a small stainless-steel bowl. Mix until well combined.

3. Pull off and discard the tough outer leaves of the artichokes and cut off the thorned tips of the remaining leaves. Turn each artichoke over so its stem is facing up and press down to open up the leaves. Return the opened artichokes to an upright position, and scrape out and discard their fuzzy chokes. Cut off and discard their stems, making sure they are flat enough on the bottom to stand upright.

4. Using a tablespoon, stuff the artichokes with the bread crumb filling, starting with the center cavity and working toward the outer leaves. Make sure to apportion equal amounts of filling to each artichoke, tamping the filling down and stuffing each artichoke as full as possible. Place the artichokes, upright and side by side, in an ovenproof, preferably glass, casserole. Add water to a depth of ½ inch. Cover the casserole with aluminum foil and bake for 1 hour. The outer leaves of the artichokes should pull off easily; if the leaves are too tough to pull off, bake for 10 minutes more.

5. Remove the casserole from the oven and uncover. Transfer the artichokes and their pan juices to a serving platter and serve hot.

~3~

· MORE ·
COMPANY

Communal Dishes for Family and Guests

{SERVING 8 TO 10}

OVERLEAF: Ricotta manicotti with roasted sweet 100s and winter herbs (pages 80–81).

Communal Tables

In my own restaurants, communal tables are one of the main features of our dining rooms. They are part of a conscious effort to hark back to the original notion of what a restaurant was meant to be, a place where public and private dining merged, where the spirit was both intimate and convivial, where everybody—including polite strangers who might become friends on the spur of the moment—felt comfortable dining *in famiglia*. You'll encounter these family-oriented scenes in many a trattoria or bistro throughout Europe, and they have become more and more popular in American restaurants in recent years.

Other than family-style recipes, the best tool for achieving a successful communal dining scenario is a big, old wooden farmhouse table. Like my Big Nonna's enameled metal table, these farmhouse tables were used not only for sitting and eating but as work surfaces. Many of them have scorch marks or nicks from cutting; all of them show a lot of individual character. I collected many different antique versions of these, and no doubt each one of them had many stories to tell. My idea was to create new stories, which would happen naturally in the course of serving my guests, many of them return customers in family groups, sharing the food and the feelings of comfort inspired by my own family traditions and memories.

We've all experienced those occasions when we've invited people over and suddenly the crowd swelled to a much bigger number than expected. This often happened at my great-grandmother's house on Sundays or holidays. Those moments used to catch me off guard, and I would feel overwhelmed, but I was always amazed at how Big Nonna never failed to put out an impressive display of food that brought everyone together and had them talking for days after. This chapter will help prepare you for those impromptu occasions when you don't think you have it in you. Occasions like these can become the glue that binds a family or social circle together—remarkable, memorable, and always worth repeating.

The vision here is of a dinner for extended family, a party of eight to twelve or more, including blood relatives, friends who are just like family, neighbors, and perhaps some last-minute guests. The recipes are designed to be served on platters and passed around a large family table. They tend toward the simple and hearty—nothing overly complicated or extra fancy—yet they never shy away from modern, inventive twists. Included are a casserole—my variation on the classic eggplant Parmesan, adding ripe peaches; a couple of satisfying meat entrées—braised veal shank (osso buco) and roasted leg of lamb; and the option of a seafood main dish (scallops). In a multicourse meal, the mussels or the manicotti could serve as the first course, perhaps after a few antipasto platters have already been enjoyed.

MUSSELS WITH CACCIATORINI, TOMATO, AND FENNEL

SERVES 8 TO 10

5 pounds wild mussels

2 tablespoons grapeseed oil

2 cups ¼-inch slivers cacciatorini
(or other small Italian dry
sausage; about ½ pound)

2 garlic cloves, thinly sliced

1 tablespoon fennel pollen (or
substitute fennel seed)

1 teaspoon red pepper flakes

One 28-ounce can pureed San
Marzano tomatoes

1 cup dry white wine

½ cup finely chopped fresh
Italian (flat-leaf) parsley

When I opened my restaurant on Nantucket in 2000, we established good relationships with a number of local seafood suppliers, one of whom was a fisherman who specialized in mussels and maintained their beds off the nearby island of Tuckernuck. It was such a thrill to have an abundance of fresh local seafood at hand all year round, but the best wild mussels were not always easy to find. (And many of their beds have since been decimated or destroyed by the red tide.) This recipe is one of my favorite preparations. It became a signature dish on our menus and we had many return customers requesting it week after week throughout the decade we owned and operated the Nantucket restaurant. Occasionally, the wild mussels would come with little tiny baby crabs inside. We taught our regular diners this was a sign of authenticity; also, since crabs are bottom feeders that clean up where they eat, it was no cause for alarm.

INGREDIENT NOTES: The most common mussels available are farm-raised P.E.I. (Prince Edward Island) mussels, which offer very little in terms of flavor. I always highly recommend the wild mussels, which bring a full, refreshing whiff of the ocean. They are definitely worth the extra step of pulling the little "beards" from their shells. Cacciatorini are the Tuscan version of a small salami- or soppressata-type dry sausage. Cacciatore means "hunter," and these little links get their name because they used to be carried around hanging from the belts of hunters and eaten as a snack while out patrolling the woods. The cacciatorini have a hint of anise flavor that, along with the fennel, works great with the mussels. If you can't locate fennel pollen, substitute the same amount of fennel seed.

TIMING NOTE: It's best to soak the mussels in salt water for at least 1 hour to give them a chance to filter out any grit.

1. Place the mussels in a large bowl or pot of cold salted water for 1 to 2 hours. Drain the water, pull the beards off the mussels, and rinse the mussels thoroughly under cold running water while rubbing or brushing their shells.

2. Place the grapeseed oil in a large 5-quart saucepan over medium heat. Add the cacciatorini, garlic, fennel pollen, and red pepper flakes. Stir well and cook for 2 to 3 minutes. Add the mussels and cook, stirring occasionally, for 2 to 3 minutes. Add the tomatoes and white wine, cover the pan, and cook until all the mussels have opened, 5 to 6 minutes more. Transfer the mussels and some of their juices from the pan to a large platter, garnish with the parsley, and serve.

STORAGE: The liquid left in the bottom of the pot can be strained and stored in a covered glass container in the refrigerator for up to 2 weeks. It can be used for a variety of seafood stews and pasta dishes.

SHAVED CELERY WITH FIGS, GORGONZOLA, HAZELNUTS, AND BALSAMIC VINEGAR

SERVES 8 TO 10

juice of 1 lemon

15 medium celery stalks

1½ pounds fresh figs, cut into quarters (dried figs can be substituted)

1 pound Gorgonzola piccante, crumbled into ½-inch pieces

1½ cups hazelnuts (about ⅔ pound), skins off, toasted and roughly chopped

½ cup extra virgin olive oil

3 tablespoons balsamic vinegar

kosher salt and cracked black pepper

This is by no means your average everyday salad. For starters, two of its main ingredients are a well-known Italian aphrodisiac: Legend has it that the combination of figs and Gorgonzola is a very effective instrument of seduction. No need to share that with the kids, but it might be an interesting fact for some of the grown-ups at your gathering. I love how the strong, complex cheese flavors, the sweetness of the figs, and the crunch of the toasted nuts contrast the freshness of the shaved celery.

TIMING NOTE: The shaved celery needs to chill in the fridge for 3 hours before you make the salad.

1. Place the lemon juice in a large stainless-steel bowl about two-thirds filled with cold water. Using a very sharp knife, cut the celery stalks on an angle into slices about 4 inches long and as thin as possible (1/16 inch), adding the slices to the lemon water immediately. When all the celery is sliced, add a tray of ice cubes to the water and place the bowl in the refrigerator for 3 hours. Remove the bowl from the fridge, transfer the celery to a large strainer or colander, and drain for 20 minutes.

2. Place the figs, Gorgonzola, and hazelnuts in another large stainless-steel bowl. Add the celery, dress the salad with the olive oil and balsamic vinegar, and toss thoroughly. Season with salt and pepper. Transfer to a large platter and serve.

PASSATO DI PEPPERONI

SERVES 8 TO 10

1 medium carrot, cut into 1-inch
   pieces

1 small Spanish onion, cut into
   1-inch cubes

2 celery stalks, cut into 1-inch
   pieces

2 tablespoons grapeseed oil

8 medium red bell peppers, cut
   in half and seeded

3 Idaho potatoes, peeled and cut
   in half (to avoid discoloration,
   hold in ice water until ready
   to cook)

2 fresh sage sprigs

2 fresh thyme sprigs

8 cups water

3 cups heavy cream

8 ounces mascarpone

kosher salt and cracked black
   pepper

2 packets of amaretti (4
   cookies), crushed, optional

During my three-month stint at Il Cibrèo, I learned how to make quite a few of the ancient Florentine specialties, including *passato, sformato,* and *al cartoccio* (see pages 32 and 146). When I returned to the United States to open my own restaurants, I was eager to create my versions of these classics. Passato in Italian means something that's been "passed through." In this case, it's a soup that's been pureed to a nice thick but smooth consistency by putting it through one of the world's greatest kitchen inventions—a good, old-fashioned, hand-operated food mill. Hearty *passato* soups are among the signature dishes of Il Cibrèo's chef, the fabulous Fabio Picchi. He makes his version of this wonderful summer soup from yellow peppers; I prefer to stick with the red, and I add my own accent with a garnish of crushed amaretti.

1. Place the carrots, onions, and celery in the bowl of a food processor with the blade attachment and process until finely chopped.

2. Place the grapeseed oil in a large 5-quart saucepan over medium heat. Add the chopped vegetables and cook, stirring occasionally, until the onions become translucent, 3 to 5 minutes. Add the bell peppers and potatoes, and continue to cook over medium heat, stirring constantly, for 5 minutes more. Add the sage and thyme, followed by the water and heavy cream, stirring well to combine all ingredients. Cook over medium heat for 45 minutes to 1 hour. Adjust the heat down to maintain a steady simmer and stir regularly so the soup doesn't burn or stick to the bottom of the pan. The soup should take on a vibrant red color and light, creamy consistency.

3. Position a food mill over another large 5-quart saucepan and pass the soup through the mill into the new pan. (Alternatively, use an immersion or stand blender.) Cook the pureed soup over medium heat for 20 minutes more, stirring regularly. Add the mascarpone and stir until it is thoroughly melted. Season with salt and black pepper; garnish with the crushed amaretti, if desired; and serve hot.

EGGPLANT AND PEACH "ALLA PARMIGIANA"

SERVES 8 TO 10

8 large eggplants, cut crosswise
into round 1½-inch-thick
slices

kosher salt and cracked black
pepper

about 3 cups extra virgin olive oil
for oiling and drizzling

10 large ripe peaches (about
5 pounds), peeled, pitted,
and cut into 1-inch-thick
slices

10 large ripe beefsteak tomatoes
(about 7½ pounds), cut into
1-inch thick slices

four 1-pound balls fresh buffalo
mozzarella, cut into ½-inch-
thick-slices

2 cups (tightly packed) fresh
basil leaves (from about
3 bunches)

2 cups fresh bread crumbs

Among my efforts to re-create the classics of Italian and Italian-American family cuisine, this is one of the more interesting and successful combinations. Though some might say it's a bit strange, you'll be very pleasantly surprised at how well it works: The sweet juices of the ripe peaches are absorbed by the eggplant, everything melts together, and all the flavors meld wonderfully hand in hand.

INGREDIENT NOTE: The eggplants should be large and firm. The peaches should be ripe and juicy. For the mozzarella, I like to use the 1-pound balls, which are about 4 inches in diameter.

1. Preheat the oven to 400°F.

2. Place the eggplant slices flat, in one layer, on 4 oiled baking sheets. Sprinkle with 1 teaspoon salt and ½ teaspoon pepper per baking sheet. Drizzle the eggplant with extra virgin olive oil and bake for 30 minutes. The eggplant slices should have a soft center. Set aside to cool.

3. On another oiled baking sheet, place a layer of slices as follows: eggplant (on the bottom), followed by peaches, tomatoes, mozzarella, and finally basil leaves. Sprinkle the top of each layer with bread crumbs and drizzle with olive oil. Repeat the whole procedure once.

4. Place the baking sheets in the oven and bake until the eggplant, peaches, tomatoes, and mozzarella have melted into one another and are soft enough to cut through easily with a knife, 40 to 45 minutes. Transfer to a large platter and serve hot.

RICOTTA MANICOTTI WITH ROASTED SWEET 100s AND WINTER HERBS

SERVES 8 TO 10 (MAKES 24 MANICOTTI)

four 1-pint containers Sweet 100 tomatoes (about 3 pounds)

1 cup extra virgin olive oil, plus more for oiling

3 garlic cloves, thinly sliced

3 tablespoons plus 1 teaspoon kosher salt

1 tablespoon plus 1 teaspoon cracked black pepper

8 tablespoons (1 stick) unsalted butter

2 cups all-purpose flour

2½ cups whole milk

2 large brown eggs

3 pounds fresh whole milk ricotta

1 cup grated Parmigiano-Reggiano

1 teaspoon red pepper flakes

½ cup finely chopped fresh rosemary leaves

½ cup finely chopped fresh sage leaves

Many people confuse cannelloni and manicotti, but there is a big distinction: Cannelloni are made using cylinders of pasta, whereas manicotti are an Italian version of crepes. Probably the main source of confusion is that both are usually stuffed with some sort of savory (and sometimes sweet-savory) filling, often ricotta based. You can create your own fillings that might include meat or fish, but this is the simple version that features a nice light consistency and represents a decidedly different take on the age-old cheese-and-tomato combination.

INGREDIENT NOTE: Of the large array of tomato varieties, Sweet 100s are among the most popular with home gardeners and indeed anybody who appreciates a small fruit with sweet, concentrated flavor. Sweet 100s are actually smaller than cherry tomatoes and get their name from the fact that their vines produce large clusters of up to 100 beautiful little fruits, only about ½ inch in diameter. If you're buying Sweet 100s instead of growing them, check your local farmers' market. If you can't find them, substitute some type of top-quality organic grape tomatoes.

TIMING NOTE: The crepes need to be made ahead of time, which could take up to 30 minutes, so take that time into consideration when preparing this dish.

1. Preheat the oven to 400°F.

2. First roast the tomatoes: Place the tomatoes, olive oil, garlic, 1 tablespoon of the salt, and 1 teaspoon of the pepper in a large stainless-steel bowl. Toss thoroughly until the tomatoes are well coated and the ingredients are well mixed. Spread the tomatoes on a baking sheet in an even layer and roast for 30 minutes. Remove from the oven and set aside to cool.

3. To make the manicotti (crepes), melt the butter in a small saucepan over medium-high heat until light golden brown, 2 to 3 minutes.

4. Place the flour, milk, eggs, and the remaining 1 teaspoon salt in a large stainless-steel bowl. Whisk until thoroughly combined. Slowly add the melted butter, whisking it in until completely incorporated. The batter should have a smooth consistency.

5. Heat a lightly oiled 6-inch nonstick sauté pan over medium heat, 1 to 2 minutes. Remove the pan from the heat and ladle about $^3/_4$ cup of the batter into the pan, evenly dispersing it around the bottom of the pan. The batter should be thin enough to see the pan through it—and the crepes should turn out to be no more than about $^1/_{16}$ of an inch thick. Place the pan back on the heat and cook for 1 minute. Use a spatula to turn the crepe over and cook for 1 minute on the other side. Carefully slide the crepes out of the pan onto a large plate to cool. Repeat the procedure until all the batter is used; you should have a total of 24 crepes (about 3 per person).

6. To make the filling, place the ricotta, Parmigiano-Reggiano, red pepper flakes, rosemary, sage, the remaining 2 tablespoons salt, and 1 tablespoon pepper in a large stainless-steel bowl. Mix thoroughly with a rubber spatula.

7. To fill the crepes, lay them flat, one at a time, and spread a large kitchen spoon of filling (about ¾ cup) toward the lower end of the crepe (the one closer to you). Fold the bottom edge up over the filling and roll the crepe away from you, gently forming and molding it into an evenly shaped cylinder. Place the crepe in a lightly oiled glass casserole. Repeat until all the crepes are filled and lined up side by side in the casserole.

8. Place the roasted tomatoes in an even layer on top of the crepes and bake uncovered for 45 minutes. Remove from the oven and serve hot, bringing the casserole to the table.

ROASTED LEG OF LAMB WITH PLUMPED APRICOTS AND GRATED RICOTTA SALATA

SERVES 8 TO 10

one 8- to 10-pound boneless leg of lamb, trimmed and tied

8 garlic cloves

4 fresh rosemary sprigs

¼ cup olive oil

1 tablespoon kosher salt

1 teaspoon cracked black pepper

4 cups brandy

2 cups dried apricots (about ¾ pound)), cut into quarters

1 cup roughly grated ricotta salata

Lamb is one of my favorite meats: I love its depth of flavor and the variety of accompaniments it suggests. Its heftiness benefits from both the sweet and acidic components in a fruit garnish. Dried apricots provide concentrated flavor, and here I add another flavor accent by plumping them up with a soaking in brandy and balancing them with a garnish of grated salty cheese. Sheep often graze in salty marshes, and authentic ricotta salata is made with at least a component of sheep's milk, further explaining the complementary nature of these flavors. I like to serve this with the asparagus on page 84.

INGREDIENT NOTE: Have your butcher trim and tie the leg of lamb if you are buying a whole leg or simply buy it already prepared from the supermarket. Fresh ricotta cheese is made from the whey (drained liquid, containing residual milk proteins) left over from a primary cheese-making process. It's soft, very mild, and lends itself to blending and enriching other ingredients, such as in cheesecakes or the filling for manicotti (see page 80). The salata version, produced mostly in Sicily and Sardinia, is salted, pressed, and aged for two to eight months, at which point it becomes hard and gratable. For this recipe, it should be roughly grated to provide a nice texture contrast.

TIMING NOTE: The lamb roasts in the oven for 1 hour and rests for 30 minutes. Meanwhile, the dried apricots are left to soak in hot brandy for 1 hour.

1. Preheat the oven to 400°F.

2. Use a paring knife to make eight 1-inch-deep slits evenly spaced into the leg of lamb. Push 1 garlic clove into each hole. Use the knife again to make four 2-inch-deep slits in the leg and fill each of those with a sprig of rosemary. Rub the lamb all over with the olive oil, and season with the salt and pepper.

3. Position the lamb on a rack in a roasting pan and roast for 1 hour. (The internal temperature should read 130–135°F on a meat thermometer; if the temperature is low, return the lamb to the oven to roast for 5 to 10 minutes more.) Remove the lamb from the oven, tent with foil, and set aside to rest for 30 minutes.

4. As the lamb begins roasting, place the brandy in a small 2-quart saucepan over medium heat for 2 to 3 minutes. Place the apricots in a stainless-steel bowl, add the hot brandy, and let the dried fruit steep for 1 hour. The brandy should be completely absorbed, and the apricots should swell in size.

5. Carve the leg of lamb crosswise into 1-inch slices, transfer to a platter, pour the apricots with their liquid on top, and garnish with the ricotta salata.

ASPARAGUS WITH FRUTTI DI BOSCO AND BROWN BUTTER

SERVES 8 TO 10

3 pounds asparagus

kosher salt

8 tablespoons (1 stick) unsalted
butter

¼ pound fresh morel
mushrooms, cut into
½-inch-thick slices

1 shallot, thinly sliced

1 cup raspberries

1 cup strawberries, quartered

2 fresh thyme sprigs

cracked black pepper

The literal translation for *frutti di bosco* is "fruits of the forest," but what it truly refers to is mixed berries, preferably of the wild kind that grow and ripen together in the woods or by the side of the road. It's a combination normally associated with desserts. Almost any classic Italian *gelateria* ("ice cream parlor") will offer a *frutti di bosco* flavor; another favorite is to serve them with a tiramisù. In this recipe, they're paired with another woodsy ingredient, the morel mushrooms, and an earthy one, the asparagus, to make a side dish that's an ideal accompaniment to roasted meat dishes like the leg of lamb recipe on page 83.

INGREDIENT NOTE: In the absence of fresh morels, you can substitute dried ones. Use ½ ounce of dried morels, which have a more intense, smoky flavor, in place of ¼ pound of fresh ones. Reconstitute the dried morels by soaking them in hot water for 20 to 30 minutes; squeeze dry, chop, and proceed with the recipe.

1. First prepare the asparagus: Trim the tough ends off the bottom of the stalks. Use a vegetable peeler to trim off the outer layer of each stalk below its spear. Bring a large pot of salted water to a boil. (Add 1 tablespoon of salt for every 2 quarts of water.) Place the asparagus in the pot, turn off the heat, and blanch for 1 minute. Drain the asparagus under cold running water to stop the cooking process and set aside. The asparagus should be just cooked through and not soft or mushy.

2. Place the butter in a large 10-inch sauté pan over medium heat. Melt until golden brown, 2 to 3 minutes. Add the morels and shallot, and cook for 3 to 4 minutes. Add the raspberries, strawberries, and thyme, stir once to combine, and cook for 2 minutes more. (Do not overstir or the sauce may become mushy.) Season with salt and pepper.

3. Transfer the asparagus to a platter and line them up so the spears are all facing in the same direction. Pour the warm mushroom-fruit mixture, along with all the melted butter from the pan, on top of the asparagus and serve.

OSSO BUCO IN RED WINE WITH ROOT VEGETABLES AND POMEGRANATE RISOTTO

SERVES 8 TO 10

ten 8-ounce pieces veal shank, cut osso buco style

2 tablespoons kosher salt, plus more to taste

1 tablespoon cracked black pepper, plus more to taste

2 tablespoons grapeseed oil

2 medium parsnips (about ½ pound), peeled and cut into 1-inch pieces

2 medium carrots, cut into 1-inch pieces

2 medium celery stalks, cut into 1-inch pieces

1 medium sweet potato, peeled and cut into 1-inch cubes

1 medium Spanish onion, cut into 1-inch cubes

1 large turnip (about 1 pound), peeled and cut into 1-inch cubes

3 fresh rosemary sprigs

3 cups dry red wine

Osso buco (literally "bone/hole") is made from large veal shanks that are cut into about two-inch-thick slices and served with a segment of bone (and its delicious marrow for scooping out). A Milanese classic usually served with risotto, the meat is braised until it's so tender you can slide it off the bone with a fork. This is my variation on the traditional recipe, adding a few ingredients you probably wouldn't find in a northern Italian kitchen. Cooking meat on the bone I find adds a touch of bitterness so I like to add a sweeter root vegetable such as parsnips and sweet potatoes. (The parsnip was native to Europe and was used in Roman times, but it was later replaced by the potato, which came from the Americas; the sweet potato was and is strictly a New World vegetable, virtually nonexistent in Europe.) The other advantage to parsnips is they're more durable than carrots, which can turn mushy after long braising. The pomegranate is a mythical, exotic, and much-prized fruit from the Near East that is also grown in southern Mediterranean climates. Its seeds add a jewellike sparkle to this dish.

TIMING NOTE: The veal shanks are browned in batches and then braised in the oven for 1 hour. While they are cooking, there is ample time to make the risotto. Don't wait too long, though, because risotto can't be rushed!

1. Preheat the oven to 400°F. Season each piece of veal shank with a generous pinch of salt and pepper.

2. Place the grapeseed oil in a large 5-quart heavy-bottomed pot or Dutch oven over medium heat. When the oil is hot, sear the veal shanks until evenly browned, 2 to 3 minutes on each side. Work in batches, leaving enough space between the shanks so they can brown nicely (and do not "boil"). Once they are browned, set the shanks aside on a plate.

3. Pour off all but about 2 tablespoons of the fat in the pot. Return the veal shanks to the pot over medium heat. Add the parsnips, carrots, celery, sweet potatoes, onions, turnip, and rosemary, and stir to combine. Add the red wine and cook until reduced by half, 3 to 5 minutes. Add 6 cups of water (or enough to cover all the ingredients) and braise in the oven for 1 hour, or until the meat easily falls away from the bone. Remove the pot from the oven and set aside.

Pomegranate Risotto

2 tablespoons grapeseed oil

2 cups finely chopped Spanish onions (from about 1 large onion)

6 cups Carnaroli rice

1 cup dry white wine

12 cups water

8 tablespoons (1 stick) unsalted butter

1 cup grated Parmigiano-Reggiano

2 cups pomegranate seeds

3 teaspoons kosher salt, plus more to taste

1 teaspoon cracked black pepper, plus more to taste

1. Put the grapeseed oil and onions in a 3-quart saucepan at room temperature. Place the saucepan over medium heat and sauté the onions, stirring occasionally with a wooden spoon, until translucent, 3 to 4 minutes. The onions should not take on any color; lower the heat if necessary. Stir the rice into the onions in the pan and toast for 1 to 2 minutes, until the kernels become opaque. While toasting, agitate the pan occasionally to keep the rice from sticking to the bottom.

2. Add the white wine, stir once, and continue to cook until it evaporates. Begin to add the water 4 cups at a time, cooking for 8 to 10 minutes after each addition. (The water will be added in three stages.) Stir the rice regularly as it releases its starch and agitate the pan occasionally to prevent sticking. Drag the spoon through the rice, and when the rice is thick enough to reveal a pathway, add the next 4 cups water and repeat the procedure. After stirring in the final portion of water, add the butter, Parmigiano-Reggiano, pomegranate seeds, salt, and pepper. Contine stirring until the cheese and butter are fully melted and the risotto attains a creamy consistency, 3 to 5 minutes more. Adjust the seasonings to taste.

3. Mound the risotto on a large platter, place the osso buco and root vegetables on top, drizzle with 1 cup of the pan juices, and bring to the table hot.

NOTE: When the risotto is done, it should have a silky appearance. The individual kernels should still be discreet and visible. The texture of a risotto should be very creamy but the grains themselves should be toothsome; they should retain some bite. You should be able to taste the featured flavor(s)—in this case subtle hints of pomegranate—not just the starchiness of the rice.

SEARED SEA SCALLOPS WITH ASPARAGUS AND RISOTTO-STYLE FRÉGOLA

SERVES 8 TO 10

4 tablespoons grapeseed oil, plus more as needed

1 cup diced Spanish onions (from 1 medium onion)

8 cups frégola

1 cup dry white wine

12 cups water

1 pound asparagus, trimmed, peeled, and cut into ¼-inch segments

4 tablespoons unsalted butter

½ cup grated Parmigiano-Reggiano

1 tablespoon kosher salt, or to taste

1 teaspoon cracked black pepper, or to taste

5 pounds sea scallops, rinsed under cold running water and patted dry

1 lemon, cut in half, seeds removed

Seared scallops are a winner on their own and a quick, special treat for larger dinner occasions. In this recipe, scallops are presented along with one very familiar ingredient, asparagus, and a not-so-familiar one, frégola. The latter is cooked risotto style by adding water in three stages, allowing the pasta to toast then cook gradually and absorb its pan liquids. Adding the frégola is a simple, straightforward step that introduces a sophisticated twist and an air of the Mediterranean islands off the coast of Italy to a couple of old favorites.

INGREDIENT NOTE: Frégola is a type of pasta made from semolina (aka durum) wheat that is formed into small pearllike balls and toasted, which gives it a characteristic nutty flavor and texture. Though it is most often associated with Sardinia, it's also popular in parts of southern Italy and has recently become an international favorite. Israeli couscous, another type of "miniature pearl" pasta, can be substituted

1. Place 2 tablespoons of the grapeseed oil in a 2-quart saucepan over medium heat. Add the onions and sauté until translucent, 3 to 4 minutes. Add the frégola and cook, stirring regularly, until it is lightly toasted, 2 to 3 minutes. Add the white wine, stir well, and cook until the wine evaporates.

2. Add 4 cups of the water to the pan and cook the frégola, stirring occasionally with a wooden spoon, until the water is absorbed. Add 4 more cups water, and continue to cook over medium heat, stirring occasionally. Once the second portion of water is absorbed, add the remaining 4 cups water and cook, stirring regularly, until the frégola is tender. The entire process should take about 20 minutes.

3. Fold the asparagus into the pan with the spoon. Add the butter and Parmigiano-Reggiano, stirring continuously until they are melted and fully incorporated, creating a creamy risotto-like consistency. Season with the salt and pepper and adjust to taste. Transfer to a large platter and cover with foil to keep warm.

4. Place the remaining 2 tablespoons grapeseed oil in a large 12-inch sauté pan over high heat. When the oil is hot, add the scallops in one layer and arrange them so they are not touching. Cook the scallops until golden brown, 2 to 3 minutes; turn them over and cook for 2 to 3 minutes more, until the other side is golden brown. Work in batches and/or use two pans as necessary. For each batch, wipe out the pan(s), add 2 fresh tablespoons of oil, and bring the pan(s) back up to heat before adding more scallops. Transfer the scallops to a warm plate, give them a generous squeeze of lemon, and cover loosely with foil to keep warm.

5. As soon as all the scallops are cooked, place them on top of the frégola, spoon the pan juices on top, and bring to the table immediately to serve.

CHOCOLATE HAZELNUT SEMIFREDDO

SERVES 10 TO 12

3 cups heavy cream, chilled

½ pound milk chocolate, roughly chopped

4 large brown eggs, yolks separated from whites, and whites reserved at room temperature

4 tablespoons sugar

½ cup strong coffee (espresso is best)

½ cup Vin Santo

2 tablespoons coffee liqueur (such as Kahlua)

1 tablespoon vanilla extract

½ pound whole milk Ricotta

¼ cup hazelnut paste

½ teaspoon kosher salt

½ cup plus 2 tablespoons sugar

2 tablespoons water

Semifreddo literally means "half cold" and is typically made by combining meringue (egg whites beaten with sugar) with an ice cream-like base to make it lighter, more airy and more akin to a frozen mousse. During our time in Alba, Piemonte, Colleen and I fell in love with the local preparations for hazelnuts. Being the sweet half of our partnership, Colleen developed a hazelnut dessert for our restaurant. Hazelnuts with chocolate are a combination that's hard to beat; adding the brittle as a garnish provides a nice texture contrast. Italians are not huge on complex desserts; they tend to emphasize simplicity and flavor. Colleen's approach certainly sticks to that tradition, and this signature dish is a great example.

INGREDIENT NOTES: Because of its higher sugar content, milk chocolate prevents the *semifreddo* from freezing too hard. My preferred brand is Caillebaut, which comes in 14-ounce bars with 30% cocoa. Hazelnut paste is available from specialty grocers (see Resources, page TK) but I recommend making your own. Most recipes include toasted hazelnuts, egg whites, confectioners' sugar, and perhaps some hazelnut liqueur. Colleen makes it from pure hazelnuts, with no added ingredients. She peels and toasts them and then purees them in a food processor. The nuts are dry and crumbly at first but after 10 to 15 minutes they will turn into a liquefied paste.

TIMING NOTE: The *semifreddo* should be left in the freezer overnight before serving. The hazelnut brittle can be made in advance and will need time to cool. Steps 6 and 7 are overlapping: #7 should be started immediately after starting #6.

1. Place 2 cups of the heavy cream in a chilled stainless-steel bowl and whip with a whisk until stiff peaks form. (The cream should be whipped while still cold; reserve the remaining 1 cup of cream in the refrigerator.) Cover the bowl with plastic wrap and chill until ready to use.

2. Line a 9 x 13-inch metal loaf pan with parchment paper, leaving enough extra paper overlapping so the top of the pan can be covered.

3. Set up a double boiler, add the chocolate to it and melt, stirring occasionally. Set aside the upper pan, covered, to keep the chocolate warm. Reserve the water in the lower pan. Place the egg yolks and granulated sugar in a large stainless-steel bowl and whisk until pale yellow. Add the espresso, Vin Santo, coffee liqueur, and vanilla extract, and stir well. Set up the double boiler, add the egg yolk mixture and cook, whisking continuously, until a thick cream forms. The mixture is ready when you can leave a trail on the sides of the bowl. Remove from the heat and set aside.

4. Place the Ricotta and hazelnut paste in the bowl of a food processor with the blade attachment and puree until thoroughly combined. Set aside.

5. Place the egg whites and salt an electric mixer with the whisk attachment. Run on medium until the egg whites begin to foam, about 2 minutes, then slowly add the 2 tablespoons of sugar. Once the whites are firm, add the hot syrup (from Step 7).

6. While the mixer is whisking the egg whites, place the $1/2$ cup of sugar and water in a small saucepan over low heat. Simmer the contents of the saucepan until completely dissolved into a smooth syrup, 3 to 4 minutes. Pour it into the egg white mixture in a slow, steady stream, with the mixer still running on medium. Once all the syrup is added, you will have a stiff meringue. Continue mixing until it cools to room temperature; this should take about 10 minutes total.

7. Place the warm melted chocolate in a large stainless-steel bowl. Using a rubber spatula, fold in the egg yolk mixture followed by the ricotta-hazelnut puree. Fold in the meringue and, finally, the chilled whipped cream. Turn the mixture over several times to ensure a smooth, thick, uniform consistency but do not overmix. Pour the *semifreddo* into the prepared loaf pan. Smooth and level the top. Cover with the overlapping parchment paper and freeze overnight.

8. Place the remaining 1 cup of heavy cream in a chilled stainless-steel bowl and whip vigorously with a whisk until stiff peaks form. If not using immediately for garnish, cover and place in the refrigerator until ready to serve.

9. Remove the *semifreddo* from the freezer 10 minutes before serving. Cut it into equal portions, place each serving on a plate, and garnish with 1 heaping tablespoon of chopped hazelnut brittle (recipe follows) and 1 large dollop of whipped cream, arranging them as you like. Store leftovers in parchment for up to 5 days.

Hazelnut Brittle

1 cup granulated sugar

$1/4$ cup hazelnuts, husks removed and toasted

1 teaspoon kosher salt

$1/2$ lemon

1. Place the sugar in an even layer in a 12-inch nonstick skillet over medium heat. Cook, stirring continuously with a wooden spoon, until dissolved and amber-brown, 6 to 8 minutes.

2. Add the hazelnuts and cook, still stirring continuously, until just incorporated into the sugar and aromatic, about 1 minute. Add the salt and stir to combine.

3. Pour the hot mixture onto a parchment-lined baking sheet and use the $1/2$ lemon to smooth it into one layer about $1/2$ inch thick. Set aside to cool to room temperature, about $1/2$ hour.

4. Once the brittle is cool, chop it roughly with a knife. It can be kept in an airtight container at room temperature for up to a week.

~4~

WEEKENDS

Fancier Recipes for Memorable Meals

{SERVING 4 TO 6}

OVERLEAF: Spring peas, lump crab arancini (pages 106–107).

The Café di Napoli Table

Colleen's grandfather Joe Piazza owned and operated his restaurant, the Café di Napoli, for more than sixty years in downtown Minneapolis. From the beginning, it served what we now know as classic Italian-American cuisine—dishes such as spaghetti and meatballs, pizza Margherita, and lots of baked pastas including lasagna, stuffed shells, cannelloni, and *mostaccioli*. Originally from Sicily, Joe was stationed in Naples during World War II. From there, he brought back a talent for making pizza as well as the inspiration for naming his restaurant. It became a regular destination for family meals and a much-beloved institution, the spot to see and be seen in the Twin Cities, Fridays through Mondays.

The Café di Napoli had a section of booths from the 1940s with pink leather wraparound seating for family-size parties. Nobody sat with his or her back to the door, and reservations were difficult to come by. Family groups would huddle around those tables as if telling secrets or conspiring, which of course is very Sicilian and added to the legend of the place. Colleen and I were lucky to inherit one of those pink booths, which we installed in our New York restaurant and which perfectly symbolized those special weekend family dinners. We had quite a few customers come in over the years and, seeing the booth, recall how some of their fondest childhood memories were of family meals at the Café di Napoli.

The weekend is a time when busy families can come together and enjoy fancier recipes that venture beyond everyday ingredients. In this day and age, when family members live farther apart from one another, weekend dinner parties are a great way to welcome them back to town if they happen to be visiting or to bring new members of an extended family into the fold, by way of a meaningful gesture: preparing a special meal.

This chapter offers recipes that may require a bit more time, but they will bring added excitement to the table and ultimately a great deal of satisfaction to both the chef and his or her guests. They are largely inspired by my time spent in Italy, where the weekends were all about going to the open markets, butchers, and bakeries to procure all the ingredients needed to prepare memorable meals, not only reflecting back on childhood memories but creating exciting new traditions.

These recipes serve four to six and feature "out of the ordinary" items such as pheasant, rabbit, cardoons, and Nantucket bay scallops. When you go the extra mile to cook with these types of ingredients, it honors your guests and makes a statement about the special nature of the meal. (Any questions or challenges you might have about procuring them will be answered in Sources, page 188.) Recipes such as Pheasant *alla Cacciatora* or the deep-fried rabbit recall specific occasions in my family dining history and invite you to create new memories each time you unveil them.

CLASSIC POLPETTINE WITH RICOTTA AND CREAMY POLENTA

SERVES 6 TO 8 (MAKES ABOUT 16 MEATBALLS)

3 pounds ground veal

2 cups whole milk ricotta

1 cup dried unseasoned
    bread crumbs

2 large brown eggs

2 garlic cloves, minced

½ cup grated Parmigiano-
    Reggiano

pinch of red pepper flakes

½ cup fresh Italian (flat-leaf)
    parsley, finely chopped

2 teaspoons kosher salt

½ teaspoon cracked black
    pepper

2 tablespoons grapeseed oil

two 28-ounce cans whole San
    Marzano tomatoes, pureed by
    passing through a food mill

Creamy Polenta (page 98)

Naturally, my Italian-American great-grandmother and grandmother made a lot of meatballs when I was growing up. But they were always from very traditional recipes: beef or pork, along with the usual grated cheese, bread crumbs, parsley, and garlic. And they always went into the sauce for the pasta. In Italy, people typically eat *polpettine* on their own, as an appetizer or entrée, without a starch. I learned to make them Florentine style at Il Cibrèo, where they add some ricotta, which lends a lighter, smoother, not-so-meaty texture. In this version, I reintroduced a starch in the form of polenta, an excellent partnership, giving the meal a northern accent.

Making polenta "from scratch" (that is, starting with cornmeal as opposed to the instant kind) is actually quite easy. One trick I use is to soak the cornmeal in water for a couple hours in advance. This softens it up and reduces the cooking time. You could call it my version of instant polenta, although it's far from instant in terms of authenticity and flavor.

INGREDIENT NOTE: In northern Italy, they make polenta from a number of different grains or flours including semolina, chickpea flour, and different grades of cornmeal. In the heart of polenta country, around Bergamo in Lombardia, they use a bit more coarsely ground cornmeal, which is how I like it.

TIMING NOTE: The meatballs bake for about ½ hour, then slowly braise for about 3½ hours. In the meantime, the polenta is soaked in water for 2 hours before cooking.

1. Preheat the oven to 400°F.

2. Combine the ground veal, ricotta, bread crumbs, eggs, one-half of the minced garlic, the Parmigiano-Reggiano, red pepper flakes, parsley, salt, and pepper in a mixing bowl. Use your hands to thoroughly mix and work all the ingredients together. Form and roll the mixture into somewhat firm meatballs 2 inches in diameter; these quantities should yield about 16 meatballs.

3. Position the meatballs 2 inches apart, so they are not touching, on a large sheet pan. Bake until they are slightly brown and firm, 30 to 35 minutes.

4. Place the grapeseed oil in a heavy-bottomed casserole or cast-iron pot over high heat. Lightly sauté the remaining garlic. Add the pureed tomatoes and 1 tomato can of water. Bring to a boil, then reduce the heat to medium. Add the meatballs and their pan juices to the pot. Bring to a simmer, reduce the heat to low, and simmer for 3½ hours. The meatballs should remain submerged to braise in the tomato sauce; add a small amount of water to the sauce if necessary.

Creamy Polenta

6 cups water, at room
    temperature

2 cups coarsely ground cornmeal
    (polenta), soaked in water
    for 2 hours in advance
    and drained

1 small garlic clove, thinly sliced

1½ teaspoons kosher salt, plus
    more to taste

about ¼ teaspoon red pepper
    flakes

3 tablespoons unsalted butter

¼ cup grated Parmigiano-
    Reggiano

PLACE THE WATER, cornmeal, garlic, 1 teaspoon of the salt, and ⅛ teaspoon of the red pepper flakes in a large saucepan over medium-high heat. Whisk continuously until the ingredients are fully incorporated and a smooth, lump-free consistency is achieved. Continue to stir. (At this point, you may want to switch from a whisk to a wooden spoon.) Continue to cook, while stirring continuously, until the polenta pulls away from the sides of the pan, 15 to 18 minutes total. Add the butter and the Parmigiano-Reggiano. Adjust the seasonings, adding salt and red pepper flakes to taste.

CARDOONS ALLA PARMIGIANA

SERVES 4 TO 6

12 cardoon stalks, washed, peeled, trimmed, and cut into sections ½ inch thick and about 3 inches long

2 tablespoons olive oil, plus more for oiling the casserole

2 garlic cloves, thinly sliced

one 28-ounce can crushed San Marzano tomatoes

1 teaspoon kosher salt, plus more to taste

¼ teaspoon cracked black pepper, plus more to taste

1 cup grated Parmigiano-Reggiano

½ cup fresh bread crumbs, toasted

Apart from the standard eggplant or chicken cutlets, there are a lot of main ingredients that work well *alla Parmigiana*. Cardoons, an unusual ingredient and one of my favorites, are among the more interesting possibilities for the "Parmesan treatment." This recipe makes for a really good, substantial side dish alongside hearty meats such as steak or lamb.

INGREDIENT NOTE: Cardoons are a member of the thistle family and related to artichokes. The edible part comes in stalks that look like very large celery. Its flavor is unique and subtle, mild but memorable and persistent, somewhat similar to artichokes. Cardoons may be difficult to find in a regular supermarket, but they are quite popular and available at farmers' markets from winter through the first part of spring. The stalks are bumpy and/or thorny—naturally because they're from the artichoke family—so they must be peeled with a vegetable peeler.

1. Preheat the oven to 400°F. Place the cardoon pieces in one layer, lined up side by side, in a lightly oiled glass casserole and set aside.

2. Place the olive oil in a medium 2-quart saucepan over medium heat. Add the garlic and cook until lightly golden around the edges. Add the tomatoes. Fill the tomato can halfway with tap water, add the water to the pan, and stir well. Raise the heat and bring the tomatoes to a boil, then lower the heat to maintain a steady simmer. Cook for 20 minutes. Add the salt and pepper. Remove the tomato sauce from the heat and adjust the seasonings.

3. Pour the tomato sauce into the casserole and spread it evenly over the cardoons. Top with the Parmigiano-Reggiano, in an even layer, then with the bread crumbs, also evenly spread. Cover the casserole with aluminum foil and place in the oven to bake for 45 minutes, or until the cardoons are fork tender. Remove the foil, bring the hot casserole to the table, and serve.

QUICK-SAUTÉED NANTUCKET BAY SCALLOPS WITH SHAVED PROSCIUTTO DI PARMA

SERVES 4 TO 6

2 tablespoons grapeseed oil,
    plus more if working
    in batches

3 pounds Nantucket bay
    scallops, rinsed and patted
    dry

1 teaspoon kosher salt

¼ teaspoon cracked black
    pepper

¼ cup dry white wine

1 tablespoon unsalted butter

8 thin slices prosciutto di Parma

Scallop season is a special time in Nantucket. The commercial window opens at the beginning of November and extends through March. Every year there seems to be a real fear about the demise of this great fishery, but thus far, the scallopers have managed to come back with a decent harvest each time. Given the sweet, delicate textures and flavors of Nantucket bay scallops, it seems a disservice to wrap them in "mere bacon." I came up with this prosciutto alternative while working on Nantucket one night. It was an improvised dish, sent out as an added treat for a group of regular customers, and it quickly established itself as a special send-out during all subsequent scallop seasons. You could say Nantucket bay are the prosciutto di Parma of scallops and vice versa.

INGREDIENTS NOTE: Nantucket bay scallops are among the most sought-after delicacies of the sea. They're smaller than sea scallops, but plumper, sweeter, and perhaps even a little nuttier tasting than other bay scallops. They are definitely worth the extra effort and expense. The alternative—such as the cultivated, farm-raised Taylor bay scallops from Cape Cod—are perfectly edible but just not up to standard. It's comparable to the difference between cultivated and wild mussels. Prosciutto di Parma is the finest type of Italian cured ham: It is the sweetest, most delicate, has a good balance of salt, and is sold sliced very thin. Any high-quality (preferably) Italian prosciutto will do, but be sure it's sliced very thin for this recipe.

1. Place the grapeseed oil in a large 12-inch sauté pan over medium heat. When the oil reaches its smoke point (you will see a light gray smoke rising), place the scallops in the pan, upright in one layer (not touching, in batches, if necessary). Season with the salt and pepper and cook the scallops until lightly browned on one side only, 2 to 3 minutes. Transfer the scallops to a large serving platter. If the pan gets messy, wipe it out and start with a fresh 2 tablespoons of oil for the next batch, making sure it is sufficiently hot before browning the remaining scallops.

2. Add the white wine to the pan, still over medium heat. Deglaze with a wooden spoon and cook until the wine is reduced by half, 2 to 3 minutes. Add the butter and stir continuously until completely melted and incorporated, 2 to 3 minutes.

3. Pour the pan sauce over the scallops and place slices of prosciutto on top in one even layer.

ALMOND-CRUSTED CHICKEN SCALOPPINE WITH WILD ARUGULA SALAD AND RICOTTA SALATA

SERVES 4 TO 6

3 cups all-purpose flour

3 large brown eggs, beaten

2 cups very finely chopped toasted almonds (use a food processor for easiest, best results)

2 cups fresh bread crumbs, toasted

about 2 tablespoons kosher salt

about 1 tablespoon cracked black pepper

3 pounds chicken scaloppine (twelve 4-ounce cutlets, each 3 x 5 inches and ½ inch thick; or 4 boneless, skinless chicken breasts, butterflied and pounded into ½-inch-thick cutlets)

¼ cup grapeseed oil

1 pound wild arugula (from about 2 large bunches), thoroughly washed, drained and spun dry

½ cup roughly grated ricotta salata

2 tablespoons extra virgin olive oil

1 lemon, cut in half and seeds removed

I love breaded chicken *scaloppine,* and they are always a hit at family dinners. Adding crushed almonds to the breading makes for a more crispy crust; the extra step of toasting the bread crumbs helps, too. This breading recipe also works well for pork chops, veal cutlets, or fish fillets. Pairing these delicious fried cutlets with a good salad is a mouth-watering combination. The lightly dressed arugula, with its fresh crunch, saltiness, and hint of lemony acidity, is a perfect complement. You could use almost any type of lettuce, but the wild arugula is great because it brings a much more interesting flavor, a little bit peppery with a pleasant suggestion of bitterness. As I've mentioned many times, including in the introduction to this book, I try to follow the Italian approach of using ingredients as seasoning agents as much as possible, and this salad is a good example of that.

1. Set up a breading station: Place the flour in one bowl, the eggs in another bowl, and the almonds and bread crumbs in a third bowl. Stir the almonds and bread crumbs well so they are thoroughly combined.

2. Season each chicken cutlet with a generous pinch of the salt and pepper. Dredge each cutlet in flour, dip it into the egg to coat, and then place it in the almond–bread crumb mixture, pressing down lightly on both sides to make sure it is well coated all over. Set the cutlet aside on a large plate and repeat until all the cutlets are breaded.

3. Place the grapeseed oil in a large 12-inch skillet over medium heat. When the oil is hot, add the cutlets to the pan in one layer, well spaced so they are not touching or overlapping. Working in batches, fry the cutlets until golden brown, 2 to 3 minutes on each side. Remove the browned cutlets to a large plate lined with paper towels and proceed with the second batch.

4. Place the arugula in a large stainless-steel bowl and sprinkle with the ricotta salata. Add the olive oil, squeeze the lemon halves into the bowl, and toss thoroughly. Arrange the cutlets on a platter and top with the arugula salad.

DEEP-FRIED RABBIT IN HONEY WITH PEPERONCINI AND SMASHED FINGERLING POTATOES

SERVES 4 TO 6

FOR THE RABBIT

4 cups whole milk

1 medium red onion, thinly sliced

1 cup (tightly packed) fresh Italian (flat-leaf) parsley leaves

one 3½- to 4-pound rabbit, cut into 6 or 8 serving-size pieces

2 cups rice flour

4 cups grapeseed oil

½ cup honey

¼ teaspoon red pepper flakes

1 tablespoon kosher salt

2 teaspoons cracked black pepper

FOR THE POTATOES

1 tablespoon plus 1 teaspoon kosher salt

2 pounds fingerling potatoes, washed and left whole

½ cup extra virgin olive oil

¼ teaspoon cracked black pepper

½ cup buttermilk

A few years back, *The New York Times* Dining section published an article about the increasing use of good honey at fine-dining establishments. It featured my recipe for deep-fried calamari, marinated in milk and served with spicy honey—pretty much the same treatment being applied to rabbit here. In Nantucket, we get lovely, pale, spring wildflower honey from a local beekeeper. Mixing hot red pepper flakes into the honey makes a sweet-spicy "dressing" and a finger-licking delicious eating experience. (Make sure to provide plenty of paper napkins when serving this one.)

Deep-frying is all about ensuring that the oil is hot enough (but not too hot) before submerging the food in it. It should be hot enough to crisp the food quickly on the outside and cook it through nicely without drying it out on the inside. The oil should not be so hot that it's bubbling or spitting; also, be sure not to introduce any drops of water, which could result in dangerous splattering. The instructions below are for deep-frying in a regular pot, preferably using a frying thermometer; if you have a deep-fryer with a built-in thermometer, so much the better.

INGREDIENT NOTE: Rabbit is butchered for cooking in a manner similar to that of chicken—into 8 serving-size pieces. The major difference, of course, is that it has four legs instead of two legs and two wings.

TIMING NOTE: The rabbit meat is marinated 4 to 6 hours in advance of cooking.

1. Place the milk, onions, and parsley in a large stainless-steel bowl. Add the rabbit pieces, cover, and place in the refrigerator to marinate for 4 to 6 hours. Remove the bowl from the fridge about 5 minutes before proceeding with step 5.

2. To make the potatoes, fill a 3-quart saucepan halfway with water, add 1 tablespoon of the salt, and bring to a boil over high heat. Add the potatoes, adjust the heat to maintain a steady boil, and cook until fork tender, about 15 minutes. Drain the potatoes, return them to the pan, and smash them with a potato masher. The potatoes should remain chunky—not mashed or stirred to a smooth puree. Add the olive oil, the remaining 1 teaspoon salt, the pepper, and buttermilk. Stir well to mix thoroughly, turn off the heat, and cover the pot to keep the potatoes warm.

3. Place the rice flour in a large bowl or dish. Pour the grapeseed oil into a large 5-quart, heavy-bottomed pot over medium heat. The pot should be large enough to contain all the oil at least 3 inches deep and not more than half full. When the oil is hot enough for frying (350–375°F), proceed with step 5. Use a candy or deep-fry thermometer to check the temperature of the oil; alternatively, test-fry a small piece of food, making sure it sizzles when submerged in the oil and begins to take on a golden color quickly. (The temperature of the oil should not exceed its smoke

on a golden color quickly. (The temperature of the oil should not exceed its smoke point, which for most cooking oils is between 420–450°F. If the oil approaches these temperatures, remove it from the heat briefly.)

4. Meanwhile, as the oil is heating, place the honey and red pepper flakes in a large stainless-steel bowl, stir to mix, and set aside.

5. Drain the milk from the rabbit pieces and pat dry. Season all over with the 1 tablespoon salt and 2 teaspoons pepper. Dredge the rabbit, onions, and parsley in the rice flour to coat well and, using tongs or a slotted spoon, carefully place them in the hot oil, 3 or 4 pieces at a time. The pieces should be entirely submerged and not touching. Use the tongs or slotted spoon to agitate the rabbit pieces occasionally as they fry. Cook until the rabbit is golden brown on the outside and white on the inside, 3 to 4 minutes. (The temperature of the oil may drop when one batch of food is placed in it to fry; allow it to return to frying temperature before starting the next batch.) Shaking off any excess oil and patting them dry with paper towels, transfer the fried rabbit, onions, and parsley leaves to the bowl with the honey and red pepper flakes, and toss thoroughly to coat well.

6. Place the smashed potatoes in one even layer on a platter and arrange the fried rabbit, onions, and parsley leaves on top.

SPRING PEAS, LUMP CRAB ARANCINI

SERVES 4 TO 6 (MAKES ABOUT 24 RICE BALLS)

4 cups plus 2 tablespoons
grapeseed oil

½ cup diced Spanish onions
(⅛-inch cubes; from about
½ medium onion)

2 cups Carnaroli rice

1 cup dry white wine

6 cups water

1 cup fresh English (or garden)
peas

1 tablespoon unsalted butter

½ cup grated Parmigiano-
Reggiano

8 ounces lump crabmeat,
fresh or pasteurized

kosher salt and cracked black
pepper

3 large brown eggs, beaten

2 cups all-purpose flour

2 cups fresh bread crumbs,
toasted

Arancini means "little oranges" in Italian and traditionally refers to a dish of rice balls, an ancient Sicilian recipe. When you coat the balls with bread crumbs and fry them, they turn a deep golden, almost orange shade. Classic *arancini* usually include either tomato sauce and/or some type of meat ragù. This version takes a completely different, much lighter approach, with crabmeat and spring peas. I've always enjoyed serving this as an appetizer for parties.

INGREDIENT NOTE: Excellent fresh-frozen peas are available all year round. I recommend using top-quality organic, tender, small spring peas.

1. Place 2 tablespoons of the grapeseed oil in a large 5-quart saucepan over medium heat. Add the onions and cook until translucent, 2 to 3 minutes. Add the rice and cook, stirring constantly, until lightly toasted, about 2 minutes. Add the white wine and cook until the wine is completely absorbed, agitating the pan regularly so that the rice doesn't stick to the bottom.

2. Add 2 cups of the water and continue cooking over medium heat, stirring occasionally, until the water is completely absorbed. Repeat this procedure twice, adding 2 cups water at a time. After adding the final 2 cups water, stir in the peas until well incorporated. Then stir in the butter and Parmigiano-Reggiano until they melt into the rice. Remove the pan from the heat, gently fold in the lump crabmeat, and season with salt and pepper. Spread the rice in an even layer on a baking sheet and set aside to cool, about 15 minutes.

3. Set up a breading station: Place the eggs in one bowl, the flour in another, and the bread crumbs in a third. Using your hands, roll about 2 tablespoons of the rice mixture into a ball about 2 inches in diameter and place it back on the baking sheet. Repeat until all the rice has been rolled into balls.

4. Place the remaining 4 cups grapeseed oil in a large 5-quart heavy-bottomed pot over medium heat. The pot should be large enough to contain all the oil at least 3 inches deep and not more than half full. When the oil is hot enough for frying (350–375°F), proceed with step 6. Use a candy or deep-frying thermometer to check the temperature of the oil; alternatively, test-fry a small piece of a rice ball, making sure it sizzles when submerged in the oil and begins to take on a golden color quickly. (The temperature of the oil should not exceed its smoke point, which for most cooking oils is between 420–450°F. If the oil approaches these temperatures, remove it from the heat briefly.)

5. Dredge each rice ball in the flour, coat with the eggs, then dredge in the bread crumbs, making sure the entire ball is well covered. Place it back on the baking sheet for safekeeping. Repeat until all the rice balls are breaded.

6. Working in batches, use tongs or a slotted spoon to carefully place the rice balls in the hot oil and fry until golden brown all over, 3 to 4 minutes. The balls should be submerged in the oil and not touching. Occasionally rotate so that they cook evenly all over. (The temperature of the oil may drop when one batch of rice balls is placed in it to fry; allow it to return to frying temperature before starting the next batch.) Transfer the fried *arancini* to a large plate lined with paper towels to drain of any excess oil, and cover with aluminum foil to keep them warm. When all the balls are fried, sprinkle with salt and serve immediately.

OLIVE OIL–POACHED FLUKE WITH GRATED RADISH AND CAPER VINAIGRETTE

SERVES 4 TO 6

2 cups olive oil

3 pounds fluke fillets, folded into 3-inch "rolls"

½ medium Spanish onion, sliced 1-inch thick

2 fresh sage sprigs, leaves only

1 tablespoon kosher salt

1 teaspoon cracked black pepper

½ cup capers, rinsed and drained

1 shallot, peeled and thinly sliced

2 fresh thyme sprigs, leaves only

juice of 1 lemon

6 radishes, washed, trimmed, and grated (medium)

Fluke, a member of the flounder family, is also known as summer flounder due to the fact that it spawns in deep ocean waters in the early spring, then moves closer to land to feed as the spring and summer progress. It's one of the most popular mild, delicate, white-fleshed fish among commercial and recreational fishermen up and down the East Coast of North America. Freshly caught fluke is one of the many seafood treats we enjoy throughout the summer months on Nantucket. The challenge, as with all fish of this nature, is to find ways to cook it so as to preserve its subtle textures and flavors. Poaching the fish in olive oil is among the best solutions—clean, simple, and guaranteed not to dry out. For me, it makes the ideal light antipasto for a warm-weather gathering. You can also apply this recipe to other white-fleshed seafood such as skate wing or trout.

INGREDIENT NOTE: For poaching, be sure to use a light, pure olive oil, not the heavier, spicier, green extra virgin type used to dress salads.

1. Place the olive oil in a shallow 12-inch sauté pan. Add the fluke, onions, sage, salt, and pepper. Bring the oil up to a simmer over medium heat, then simmer for 2 to 3 minutes. Remove from the heat and set aside, leaving the fluke in the oil in the pan.

2. Place the capers, shallots, thyme, ½ cup of the olive oil from the pan, and the lemon juice in a blender. Blend at medium speed for 2 minutes to make a dressing with a chunky consistency.

3. Transfer the fluke and onions from the pan to a platter, discarding the oil. Place about 1 tablespoon of the caper dressing on top of each fillet, garnish with the grated radish, and serve.

PHEASANT ALLA CACCIATORE

SERVES 4 TO 6

2 tablespoons grapeseed oil

one 8-pound pheasant, cut into
6 or 8 serving-size pieces

2 tablespoons kosher salt

1 tablespoon cracked black
pepper

2 medium carrots, cut into
1-inch pieces

1 medium Spanish onion, cut
into 1-inch cubes

2 medium celery stalks, peeled
and cut into 1-inch segments

1 cup pitted black Cerignola
olives (about ½ pound)

½ cup capers, rinsed and
drained

½ pound cacciatorini sausage,
cut into 1-inch cubes

2 fresh rosemary sprigs

1 cup dry red wine

one 28-ounce can crushed San
Marzano tomatoes

4 cups water

Creamy Polenta (page 98)

One year, my grandmother was visiting us on Nantucket for the holidays and we wanted some type of stew for our New Year's Day family dinner. I had a pheasant in the freezer and lingering thoughts of serving it over creamy polenta. She used to make an excellent chicken cacciatore, and I decided to make this as an ode to her dish. (Everybody liked it; it brought us a sense of comfort.) I put in some familiar ingredients, added a little dry sausage to liven things up, and came up with this interesting version of the *cacciatore* ("hunter-style") preparation, which works really well with this game-bird meat. Creamy Polenta (page 98) is a highly recommended accompaniment to this hearty, delicious meal for any family occasion.

INGREDIENT NOTE: See the note about cacciatorini sausage on page 72.

1. Preheat the oven to 400°F.

2. Place the grapeseed oil in a large 5-quart pot or Dutch oven over medium heat. Season the pheasant with the salt and pepper and, working in batches if necessary, brown it in the pot, 2 to 3 minutes per side. Remove the pheasant from the pot and set aside.

3. Add the carrots, onions, and celery to the pot and cook over medium heat, stirring occasionally, until the onions are translucent, 2 to 3 minutes. Add the olives, capers, cacciatorini, and rosemary, and stir. Add the red wine and continue to cook until the wine is reduced by half, 6 to 8 minutes. Add the tomatoes and water, raise the heat, and bring to a boil. Cover the pot and place it in the oven to braise until the meat falls off the bone, 45 minutes to 1 hour. The liquid should reduce by half. Transfer to a large platter and serve with the Creamy Polenta.

CIPOLLINE IN AGRODOLCE

SERVES 4 TO 6

2 tablespoons grapeseed oil

2 pounds cipolline (pearl onions can be substituted)

1 fresh rosemary sprig

1 teaspoon kosher salt, plus more to taste

¼ teaspoon cracked black pepper, plus more to taste

½ cup balsamic vinegar

Agrodolce is the Italian term for "sweet and sour." Most of the Italian recipes that include a sweet-and-sour sauce employ vinegar and sugar to achieve the balance. They are believed to have originated in ancient Sicily, brought up from northern Africa during one of the waves of Arab conquest. Despite their pungent character, onions—particularly the small ones known as *cipolline* (the diminutive of the word *onion, cipolla*)—contain plenty of natural sugars so there's no need for added amounts of that. Some recipes call for sugar or even brown sugar, but I don't feel this is necessary, as long as you execute the key first step properly: Take a few minutes to make sure those onions are browned all over, stirring all the while, so they are nicely caramelized, releasing all their sugars into the pan. Then stir in the balsamic vinegar, which has its own built-in component of sweetness, and you have a delectable balance. You can chop up the *cipolline* and use this recipe as a topping for *crostini*. It could also serve as a condiment or, with the onions left whole, as an appetizer or side dish for main courses such as the Pheasant *alla Cacciatore* opposite.

INGREDIENT NOTE: *Cipolline* are small, flattish, sweet onions, 1 to 3 inches in diameter, once grown only in Italy, but now are much more common and available in many American markets. In a pinch, regular pearl onions can be substituted.

PLACE THE GRAPESEED oil in a large 12-inch skillet over medium heat. Add the *cipolline* and rosemary sprig. Cook the onions for 8 to 10 minutes, stirring and turning regularly to ensure that they brown well all over. Lower the heat if the onions threaten to blacken. Season with the salt and pepper. Add the balsamic vinegar and continue to cook, stirring so the onions don't stick, until the vinegar is reduced by half, 2 to 3 minutes. Adjust the seasonings. Transfer the onions and their pan juices to a platter and serve hot.

CLASSIC CASSATA

SERVES 4 TO 6

1 pint strawberry gelato,
softened (left at room
temperature for about
20 minutes)

1 pint chocolate gelato, softened

1 pint vanilla gelato, softened

4 ounces unsweetened
chocolate, roughly chopped

8 ounces bittersweet chocolate,
roughly chopped

⅓ cup corn syrup

½ cup plus 1 cup heavy cream

1 pint strawberries, washed,
trimmed, and cut into quarters

A traditional Sicilian cassata, which originated in the area around Palermo, is made by layering a rum-soaked sponge cake with sweetened ricotta. The term *cassata* implies a "marriage" of layers. There is also a version from Sulmona, Abbruzzi, layered with praline and pound cake. This is Colleen's interpretation of one of the more famous contemporary variations on a cassata: a frozen layered ice cream cake. It was born out of our desire to utilize the bounty of fresh goat milk we had on Nantucket. What could be more delicious and comforting than vanilla, chocolate, and strawberry ice cream all rolled into one dessert. It's been family tested and approved many times.

INGREDIENT NOTES: For the bittersweet chocolate, I recommend Caillebaut, or an equivalent high-quality product such as Valrhona, with 70% cocoa or higher. For the unsweetened chocolate, you can use baker's chocolate (same brands). Gelato, of course, is Italian for ice cream, but there are several major differences between authentic Italian-style ice cream and the commercial brands popular in the United States. *Gelato* is churned at a lower speed, pumping less air into it, and therefore is more dense, with richer, more concentrated flavor, than regular American ice cream. It doesn't coat the tongue so much, which also allows you to taste more flavor. *Gelato* also contains less butterfat, which means it can be frozen at a higher temperature and therefore, somewhat paradoxically, it has a smoother, creamier mouth-feel. Due to these properties, *gelato* has a much shorter shelf-life—it can only be stored frozen for a few days—and is generally made and served, artisan-style, on the premises of a gelateria.

TIMING NOTE: The procedure outlined in step 1 for softening the three flavors of ice cream, then refreezing them, will take a total of more than 3 hours on the first day; so it is something to plan while you're multitasking other kitchen projects or almost anything else around the house. The remaining steps—making the icing, applying it, and allowing it to set in the freezer—are done the next day.

1. Line a 9 x 13-inch metal loaf pan with parchment paper, making sure there is enough extra paper overlapping so the top of the pan can also be covered. Spread the strawberry gelato in one even layer in the bottom of the loaf pan using an offset spatula. Place the pan in the freezer for 1 hour or until the gelato is well frozen. Remove the pan from the freezer and repeat the process with the chocolate gelato, spreading it in an even layer on top of the strawberry layer. Then repeat the same process to form a third layer of vanilla gelato. Return the cassata to the freezer for at least 8 hours or overnight. Be sure to cover the layers of gelato each time by folding the overlapping parchment paper over the top of the loaf pan.

2. Place the unsweetened chocolate and bittersweet chocolate in a medium stainless-steel bowl. Place the corn syrup and $1/2$ cup heavy cream in a large saucepan over medium-high heat and bring to a boil. Be careful the mixture does not over-boil; if it starts to bubble violently, lower the heat. When the mixture comes to a boil, pour it immediately into the bowl with the chocolate, stir until well combined into a smooth, shiny, thick consistency, then let stand for 5 minutes.

3. Remove the cassata from the freezer. Unfold the overlapping paper and, using the slack, carefully lift the cassata out of the pan. Unwrap it from the parchment paper and carefully transfer it to a parchment-lined sheet pan or large plate; the pan or plate should be small enough to fit in your freezer. Working quickly with an offset spatula, begin spreading the chocolate icing in an even layer $1/2$ inch thick to cover the three exposed sides of the cassata. Meanwhile, keep the chocolate mixture warm in the double boiler. Place the cassata back in the freezer until the chocolate has hardened, about 30 minutes. Remove the cassata from the freezer, carefully rotate it 90 degrees, and coat its underside with chocolate. Place the cassata back in the freezer for 1 hour.

4. Place the 1 cup heavy cream in a chilled stainless-steel bowl and whip vigorously with a whisk until stiff peaks form. If not using immediately, cover and place in the refrigerator until ready to serve.

5. Using a sharp, hot knife, slice the cassata crosswise into 1-inch-thick portions, place each portion on a plate, and garnish with a large dollop of whipped cream and some fresh strawberries.

~5~

SUNDAYS

Traditional Recipes for Sunday Family Meals

{SERVING 6 TO 8}

OVERLEAF: Goat milk panna cotta with macerated cherries and ginger biscotti (pages 136–138).

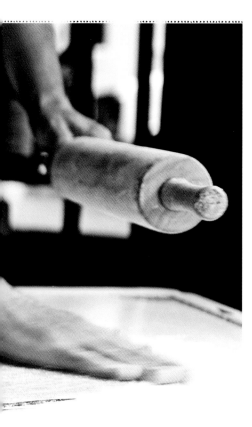

Big Nonna's Table

My first memories of learning to cook are dominated by being around my great-grandmother's kitchen table. Not only did we eat many of our family dinners there but she used it as a work area for prep as well, sprinkling flour and rolling out the dough for her fresh pasta or *pizza rustica* right on the surface. It was truly a centerpiece and hub for our entire family. For example, after I had it shipped to our restaurant in Nantucket, I unwrapped it, examined it, and realized it was covered with little scraps of Scotch tape. Puzzled, I called my mom to ask her if she had any clue about these. She explained that when my sisters and I were little we would tape our construction paper and coloring books to the table to keep them steady before we went at them with our crayons.

Big Nonna's table has wooden legs and a metal top with a white enamel surface. The top has a lip around its edges and a blue frieze pattern, making it both practical for work and decorative for dining. It's amazing how a sturdy, utilitarian object like this can come to symbolize so much in a person's life. It can become so beautiful in your mind's eye. That's exactly how I feel about this table, and I'm happy I still have it to share with my family.

This chapter highlights recipes inspired by a strong element of family tradition—from memories of my great-grandmother's Christmas Eve seafood meals to Sunday-afternoon dinners for the entire family at my grandmother's; from the Piazza family's caponata, a Sicilian staple, to my grandmoter's creamed corn, a treasured personal recollection. For me, it started relatively early in life: When I was about eight, my mother, grandmother, and great-grandmother recognized my enthusiasm for cooking. Sometimes before a Sunday family dinner, my grandmother picked me up at home early and drove me over to Big Nonna's so I could help them get started. We looked forward to these Sunday family meals the whole week leading up to them, and they kept us going for days after.

These are meals meant to serve six to eight, for those occasions when there's ample time to enjoy preparing and consuming a feast in leisurely fashion and when the goal is to develop a shared feeling of abundance among all the members of your immediate and extended families. The recipes are classics of our Italian family heritage that, at the same time, have become my own signature dishes. Passing recipes like these down from generation to generation is one of the best ways to uphold family traditions. I hope the recipes here inspire you to preserve your family's traditions and also create new ones to pass down to the next generation.

COLLEEN'S "FAMOUS" BREAD

YIELDS 1 LOAF, 16 X 6 INCHES

FOR THE STARTER

1 cup (about 6 ounces)
   all-purpose flour

1 cup (about 6 ounces)
   whole wheat flour

1½ cups filtered water

FOR THE DOUGH FERMENT

1⅛ cups all-purpose flour

¼ teaspoon kosher salt

⅛ teaspoon active dry yeast

½ cup filtered water

FOR THE BREAD

3 cups all-purpose flour, plus
   about ½ cup for flouring

⅛ teaspoon active dry yeast

1 tablespoon kosher salt,
   plus about ½ teaspoon
   for sprinkling

1 cup dough ferment

½ cup starter

2 tablespoons extra virgin olive
   oil, plus 1 teaspoon for oiling

1½ cups filtered water

When Colleen and I decided to open our restaurant in Nantucket, bread was the last thing on our minds. Then, about six weeks before opening, we realized that neither of us had any real experience with bread baking. Yet we were determined to offer our own exceptional take on this all-important family staple. So we contacted a few friends in New York City and were able to arrange a three-day *stage* at Balthazar, where they offer a variety of wonderful homemade-style breads. When we got back to our kitchen, Colleen began experimenting with starters and quickly created an acceptable basic recipe. She worked hard over the ensuing months to perfect it and eventually developed this beautiful rustic country-style bread with a silky soft crumb and crispy crust; it soon attracted a cult following.

I admit that this involves a fairly drawn-out process, but I guarantee the results are worth the effort. You might find a comparable fresh bread in a store, but I bet you won't find anything better. Follow this recipe closely, but then feel free to tweak it and create your own version. And remember, always have patience: Bread dough can be temperamental, and the first time is not always the charm.

TIMING NOTE: If you want bread this good, there really aren't a lot of shortcuts. The starter, which we keep going year-round, is begun at least four days before you make the dough. The dough ferment, which is the second crucial step, is prepared the day before and refrigerated overnight; once you have one bread made, a portion of the dough becomes the dough ferment for the next batch. The dough requires two extensive rising periods: The first one is up to 24 hours and the second 2 hours on the day you plan to bake the bread.

1. First prepare the starter: Place the all-purpose flour, whole wheat flour, and water in a stainless-steel bowl and, using a wooden spoon, stir to combine thoroughly; the mixture will have the consistency of thick pancake batter. Store the starter in a nonreactive container (glass, ceramic, or plastic), covered in cheesecloth, at room temperature for about 4 days. Once a day, stir it with a wooden spoon to mix thoroughly. Every other day, discard half the starter, replenishing it with the same amount of the mixture in equal parts all-purpose flour, whole wheat flour, and water. Maintain the consistency by adjusting the quantity of water as necessary. The starter is ready to use when it begins to bubble and grow.

2. To prepare the dough ferment, combine the flour, salt, yeast, and water in a stainless-steel bowl. Stir with a wooden spoon until the mixture attains the consistency of a sticky dough. Cover the bowl with a dish towel and leave out overnight at 65°F. The ferment should be bubbly and risen when complete.

3. To make the bread, combine the 3 cups flour, yeast, salt, dough ferment, starter, 2 tablespoons of olive oil, and the water in the large bowl of an electric mixer with the paddle attachment. Beat on medium-high speed until the dough peels away from the sides of the bowl, about 10 minutes. Turn off the mixer and allow the dough to rest for 20 minutes. Beat for another 5 to 10 minutes until the dough is shiny.

4. Oil the inside of a nonreactive rectangular (about 16 x 9 x 6 inches) container large enough for the dough to double in size. Transfer the dough to the container and cover tightly with a lid or place in a food-grade plastic bag. The dough should not stick to the sides of the container.

5. Place the dough in a cool (about 65°F) place and allow it to rise for 18 to 24 hours. If the dough has not begun to rise after about 2 hours, move it to a warmer location; it must double in size to proceed with the recipe.

6. Sprinkle the additional $1/2$ cup flour onto a dry work surface (the dough is wet, so flour generously). Carefully pour the dough onto the floured surface so as to avoid deflating it. Using a bench scraper, cut off 1 cup of the dough and save it as the dough ferment for the next batch of bread. (It can be stored in an airtight container in the refrigerator for up to 3 days or in the freezer for up to 2 months.)

7. With well-floured hands and a very light touch so as to deflate the dough as little as possible, roll it into a cylindrical loaf about 3 x 6 inches. Line a 13 x 9-inch baking sheet with parchment paper and brush with olive oil. Carefully place the dough in the center of the baking sheet. Place the sheet inside a food-grade plastic bag, covering the dough and tying or sealing the bag shut. Allow to rest in a warm spot (about 70°F) until doubled in size, about 2 hours.

8. Preheat the oven to 500°F. Place a large skillet or baking stone in the oven for at least 30 minutes to heat it up. If using a skillet, it should be placed upside-down.

9. Carefully slide the bread dough with its parchment paper onto the heated baking stone or skillet. Once the door is closed, lower the heat to 400°F. Bake until golden brown, about 30 minutes. After 15 minutes, rotate the pan 90 degrees.

10. Remove the bread from the oven and paint it with about 1 teaspoon olive oil and sprinkle with about $1/2$ teaspoon sea salt. Allow the bread to rest for at least 1 hour before serving.

SERVING: The crust will soften as it cools. To crisp the crust before serving, reheat the bread at 400°F for 10 minutes.

STORAGE: The bread will stay fresh in a bread box at room temperature for about 2 days. Wrapped tightly in plastic, it can be frozen for up to 2 weeks.

POACHED BACCALÀ SALAD

SERVES 6 TO 8

3 pounds salt cod, soaked in
   water 24 hours in advance
   (change water every 6 to
   8 hours)

½ gallon (8 cups) whole milk

1 bay leaf

2 celery stalks, diced
   (¼-inch cubes)

1 red bell pepper, diced
   (¼-inch cubes)

½ cup finely chopped fresh
   Italian (flat-leaf) parsley

½ cup extra virgin olive oil

juice of 1 lemon

kosher salt and cracked
   black pepper

The inspiration for this recipe comes from my great-grandmother Big Nonna: Every year for our Christmas Eve *sette pesci* ("seven fishes") dinner, she would make a scungilli salad. Scungilli (whelk) is not all that popular and can be difficult to find except in Italian or Chinese specialty markets. Baccalà, however, is widely available all year round (since it's preserved by salt curing). This dish can be served as an antipasto on its own or as a topping for a leafy green salad.

TIMING NOTE: Aside from soaking the salt cod in fresh water for a day in advance, this is a quick, simple recipe suitable for many different occasions.

1. Place the salt cod, milk, and bay leaf in a medium heavy-bottomed sauce pan over medium heat and bring to a light simmer. Continue to simmer for about 10 minutes until the cod flakes easily.

2. Remove the pan from the heat and allow the cod to soak in the milk as it cools to room temperature, about 30 minutes. Discard the bay leaf.

3. Combine the celery, bell pepper, and parsley in a medium stainless-steel mixing bowl. Using a fork, flake the cooled salt cod in bite-size pieces into the bowl with the vegetables; stir well to mix. Dress the salad with the olive oil and lemon juice. Toss, then season with salt and pepper. Serve chilled.

ROASTED RED BELL PEPPERS WITH GOLDEN RAISINS IN BALSAMIC VINEGAR

SERVES 6 TO 8

6 large red bell peppers

1 cup olive oil

¼ cup balsamic vinegar

½ cup golden raisins

2 fresh thyme sprigs, leaves only, minced

kosher salt and cracked black pepper

This is another quick, easy, and versatile preparation that stores easily (in a jar or covered container) and keeps well. It's a good idea to have some of these peppers on hand at all times. I love the way the sweet and sour flavors in this recipe play off one another, leaning a bit toward the sweet. For your antipasto course, they are a great accompaniment to cheeses or cured meats (balancing their drier, saltier character), or just by themselves on a piece of good crusty bread. They make a fine side dish or garnish for almost any meal and work very well inside sandwiches.

1. Preheat the oven to 400°F.

2. Position the red bell peppers upright in a medium casserole, trimming the bottoms flat if necessary. Drizzle each bell pepper with 1 tablespoon of the olive oil. Bake the bell peppers until their skins blister, 45 minutes to 1 hour.

3. Remove the casserole from the oven and set aside at room temperature. When the bell peppers are cool enough to handle, peel and discard their skins. Scoop out and discard all seeds and stems from their insides, then, with your fingers, tear the bell peppers lengthwise (from bottom to stem) into ½-inch strips.

4. Place the roasted pepper strips, the remaining olive oil, the balsamic vinegar, golden raisins, and thyme in a nonreactive mixing bowl. Season with salt and pepper, and stir to mix well. Allow to marinate for 2 hours at room temperature, then serve.

STORAGE: The bell peppers can be kept in a covered nonreactive container in the refrigerator for up to 2 weeks. Bring to room temperature before serving.

THE PIAZZA FAMILY SICILIAN CAPONATA
WITH CORNMEAL CRACKERS

SERVES 6 TO 8

1 cup grapeseed oil

1 red bell pepper

1 cup diced Spanish onions,
 (¼-inch cubes, from
 ½ medium onion)

½ cup salt-cured capers, rinsed
 and drained

½ cup diced black olives
 (⅛-inch pieces)

3 large eggplants, peeled and
 cut into ½-inch cubes

¼ cup red wine vinegar

kosher salt and cracked black
 pepper

Colleen's mother's family comes from Sicily, which is also where caponata originated. One of its main ingredients, capers, are indigenous to the island and turn up in many of the best Sicilian recipes. Colleen's Grandpa (Joe) Piazza, who started out as a cook, spent time perfecting his versions of many such classics, which were served for years at his restaurant in downtown Minneapolis, the famous Café di Napoli, and passed down through the family. Every year, Colleen's parents gather their garden vegetables, and this is one of their favorite recipes to jar and share with family and friends. For an antipasto or side dish, it's really hard to beat a good caponata: Its flavors are both smoothly subtle and deeply satisfying; the overall effect is deliciously addictive. I added the crackers to provide a vehicle for this ambrosia, contributing some nice contrasting crunch and allowing it to be served as a canapé.

1. Place the grapeseed oil in a heavy-bottomed braising pan over medium heat. Add the bell pepper, onions, capers, and black olives and lightly sauté, stirring occasionally with a wooden spoon, until the onions are translucent, about 8 minutes.

2. Add the eggplant and continue to cook over medium heat for an additional 20 minutes, stirring every 5 minutes. The eggplant should become soft and translucent.

3. Remove the pan from the heat, stir in the vinegar, and season with salt and pepper. Mix thoroughly and serve.

STORAGE: The caponata can be kept covered in the refrigerator for up to 2 weeks. Bring to room temperature before serving.

Cornmeal Crackers

SERVES 6 TO 8

1 cup all-purpose flour

1 cup fresh stone-ground cornmeal

1 teaspoon kosher salt, plus more for sprinkling

5 black peppercorns, crushed

3 tablespoons sugar

1 teaspoon baking powder

½ cup whole milk

4 tablespoons unsalted butter, melted

1 teaspoon finely chopped shallots

1 teaspoon finely chopped fresh thyme leaves

1. Preheat the oven to 400°F.

2. Combine the flour, cornmeal, salt, peppercorns, sugar, and baking powder in a large mixing bowl.

3. Place the milk, butter, shallot, and thyme in a blender at medium speed or the bowl of a food processor with the blade attachment and blend/process for about 2 minutes, or until well incorporated.

3. Pour the milk mixture from the blender/processor into the flour mixture and work the two together with your hands, kneading the dough with your fingers, until a pliable dough forms.

4. Use a rolling pin to roll the dough out between the 2 sheets of parchment paper to a thickness of ¼ inch. Place the bottom parchment with the dough cylinder on a baking sheet. Sprinkle the dough with about 1 teaspoon salt and bake for 8 to 10 minutes, or until golden around the edges.

5. Remove the dough from the oven and cut it into 2-inch squares or, if you prefer, diagonal shapes. (There is no need to separate them at this stage; they will easily break apart once fully baked.) Return the crackers to the oven and bake until golden brown, 10 to 15 minutes. Allow to cool to room temperature and serve.

STORAGE: The crackers keep in an airtight container at room temperature for up to 2 weeks.

BRAISED SHORT RIBS WITH GIARDINIERA AND SPRING HERBS

SERVES 6 TO 8

12 short ribs of beef

kosher salt and cracked black pepper

¼ cup grapeseed oil

1 medium Spanish onion, chopped (¼-inch pieces)

3 medium carrots, chopped (¼-inch pieces)

2 celery stalks, chopped (¼-inch pieces)

1 medium fresh rosemary sprig

2 cups dry red wine

6 fresh thyme sprigs

6 fresh chive blossoms

Giardiniera (page 127)

Braised short ribs are featured in many family-style cuisines all over the world. No wonder: They're ideal for large parties, and they lend themselves to spending less time in the kitchen and more time with your guests. This is no light, eat-on-the-run summer fare but rather the centerpiece of a long, leisurely sit-down with the entire extended family.

Good meaty, bone-in short ribs weigh about a third of a pound each. Ask your butcher for English-cut style, which are separated into 2- to 3-inch cubes, each with a piece of the bone attached. Braised short ribs are a prime example of how long, slow cooking of tougher cuts of meat on the bone yields deep flavors and succulent textures. I like to garnish them with fresh herbs and serve a *giardiniera* on the side. The lip-smacking vinegary flavor of the pickled vegetables works well in contrast to the heft of this hearty main dish.

TIMING NOTE: Both of these recipes can be made well in advance. The braised ribs make for excellent leftovers, simply reheated on their own or combined with some tomato sauce to make a quick ragu for pasta.

1. Preheat the oven to 400°F.

2. Season the short ribs with salt and pepper. Place the grapeseed oil in a large 5-quart, heavy-bottomed stockpot or Dutch oven over high heat. The oil should lightly smoke so you know it's hot. Cook each rib until golden brown all over, about 2 minutes per side, then set aside.

3. Pour the grease out of the pot, then put all the ribs back in, along with the onions, carrots, celery, and rosemary sprig. Add the red wine and bring to a boil over high heat, stirring with a wooden spoon to deglaze the bottom of the pot. Adjust the heat to maintain a steady boil and cook until the wine is reduced by half, 6 to 8 minutes.

4. Add enough water to cover the ribs, increase the heat to high, and bring the liquid to a boil. Cover the pot and place it in the oven to braise for up to 1 hour, or until the meat is tender and separating from the bone.

5. Remove the pot from the oven and allow the ribs to rest in their braising liquid for about 20 minutes. Place the ribs and vegetables on a serving platter, drizzle with their pot liquor, and garnish with thyme sprigs, chive blossoms, and Giardiniera.

Giardiniera

SERVES 6 TO 8

1 head cauliflower, small florets
only

1 red bell pepper, julienned

1 celery stalk, julienned

1 large carrot, julienned

1 Spanish onion, thinly sliced

1 pound green beans, trimmed
and cut into 1½-inch pieces

1 bay leaf

1 cup white wine vinegar

kosher salt and cracked black
pepper

The point of the cooking process here is to just bring the fresh vegetables to a boil then allow them to steep in their cooking liquid so they absorb plenty of the vinegar flavor yet still retain a nice hint of their fresh crunch. *Giardiniera* is the feminine of "gardener"—a more complete or descriptive translation might be "pickled salad of fresh garden vegetables."

1. Place the cauliflower, bell pepper, celery, carrot, onion, green beans, bay leaf, and vinegar with 6 cups water in a large 5-gallon, stainless-steel stockpot over high heat. Bring to a boil, lower the heat, and simmer for 8 to 10 minutes.

2. Remove the pot from the heat and let the vegetables steep in their liquid for 1 hour. Season the *giardiniera* with salt and pepper. When it has cooled to room temperature, transfer to a nonreactive container with enough of the liquid to cover the vegetables by ½ inch, cover the container with a lid or plastic wrap, and refrigerate until ready to serve.

STORAGE: The giardiniera can be kept in the refrigerator for up to 2 weeks. Bring to room temperature before serving.

CREAMED CORN WITH MASCARPONE AND BLACK PEPPER TARALLI

SERVES 6 TO 8

2 tablespoons grapeseed oil

1 medium Spanish onion, diced (⅛-inch cubes)

6 cups fresh corn kernels cut off the cob

4 cups whole milk

8 ounces mascarpone

kosher salt and cracked black pepper

Black Pepper Taralli (opposite page)

Here is a recipe inspired by a fond childhood memory: When I was in grade school, my grandmother used to pick me up, take me to her apartment, and serve me some delicious snacks. One of my favorites was warmed-up leftover creamed corn garnished with crushed black pepper *friselle*, which look like stretched or flattened bagels, and are hard and crunchy like croutons. Most people buy this very typical southern Italian product at traditional Italian groceries because making it involves a two-stage baking process. The black pepper *taralli* in this combo are a nod to the *friselle* my grandmother fed me, but more compact and less complicated to make.

INGREDIENT NOTE: *Mascarpone* is a very rich (triple cream), spreadable cheese that originated in the outskirts of Milan in Lombardy. It's often used in desserts and/or fillings. I like it as a thickener for soups, risottos, and other dishes where a creamy consistency is the goal. Its flavor is very mild so its main contribution is its richness.

1. Place the grapeseed oil in a large 5-quart, heavy-bottomed saucepan over medium heat. Add the onions and sauté, stirring occasionally, for about 5 minutes, or until they become translucent. Add the corn and continue to cook, stirring regularly, for another 5 to 7 minutes.

2. Add the milk and 4 ounces of the mascarpone. Stir constantly until the mascarpone is melted. Lower the heat to a simmer and cook for about 30 minutes.

3. Remove half of the corn mixture from the pan and place it in a blender. Puree on medium-high. Return the puree to the pan and stir well to incorporate. Season with salt and pepper, garnish each portion with a dollop of the remaining mascarpone, and serve hot with the taralli.

Black Pepper Taralli

MAKES 3 DOZEN

2½ teaspoons active dry yeast

1 cup warm water

½ cup extra virgin olive oil, plus
more for brushing

3½ cups all-purpose flour, plus
1 to 2 tablespoons more
for flouring

1 tablespoon kosher salt

2 tablespoons coarsely cracked
black pepper

2 tablespoons fennel seeds,
crushed

Taralli are southern Italy's answer to pretzels. Actually they're more like a cross between a pretzel and a bagel and, in fact, one traditional recipe involves a two-step cooking process of boiling then baking them the way bagels are made. *Taralli* can be sweet or savory. They're an all-purpose snack, nice to have around at the beginning of a meal and also at the end, and they are frequently enjoyed dipped in wine. My mother often made them from scratch; I got this recipe from her and developed it for my restaurant.

TIMING NOTE: The dough has a 1- to 2-hour rising period.

1. Preheat the oven to 350°F.

2. Combine the yeast, water, and olive oil in a large stainless-steel bowl and stir well. Cover with a dish towel and set aside at room temperature for 10 to 12 minutes.

3. Place the flour, salt, pepper, and fennel seeds in another large stainless-steel bowl and stir until well combined. Add the flour mixture to the yeast mixture, combining them by hand and kneading until a soft dough is formed. Place in a clean, oiled stainless-steel bowl, cover, and set aside at room temperature to rise for 1 to 2 hours.

4. Place the dough on a floured work surface and cut it into 6 pieces. Roll each piece into a log approximately ½ inch in diameter. Cut the logs into 3-inch segments and form each segment into a ring or knot. Line 2 baking sheets with parchment paper and place the rings on the sheets 1 inch apart. Bake for 30 minutes.

5. Remove the sheets from the oven and lightly brush the *taralli* with olive oil. Return the taralli to the oven to bake for 10 minutes more, or until golden in color. Let cool before serving.

STORAGE: Taralli can be kept in an airtight container at room temperature for up to 2 weeks.

ORATA SOTTO SALE WITH CREAMED FENNEL AND PRESERVED LEMONS

SERVES 6 TO 8

6 large brown egg whites

2 pounds kosher salt

2 teaspoons grapeseed oil

4 whole orata (dorade), about 3 pounds each, cleaned and gutted

Lemon wedges for garnish

Creamed Fennel (page 132)

Preserved Lemons (page 133)

On my very first trip to Italy with Colleen, we worked for Danilo Lorusso at his Ristorante La Crota in Roddi, near Alba, Piemonte, during truffle season. He couldn't afford to pay us, but we left rich in experiences. As my birthday present, Danilo sent us to a friend of his who had a family bed-and-breakfast in Savona, on the Ligurian coast between Genoa and San Remo. There, they did a lot of great things with seafood, including a whole salmon cooked under a salt crust (*sotto sale*)—the first time we'd seen this method. The *padrone* presented it on a platter, broke open the crust, and lifted the tender fillets right onto our plates, serving them with roasted potatoes and pesto.

Baking "under salt" is one of the best ways of keeping fish, particularly the delicate-fleshed varieties, moist and flavorful. This recipe calls for orata (known as dorade or royal dorade in French), which is a species of bream native to the Mediterranean. Red snapper, striped bass, branzino (Mediterranean sea bass), or any other white-fleshed fillet fish can be substituted.

TIMING NOTE: The Creamed Fennel takes about 25 minutes to cook, depending on your desired consistency. Start it first then, once it's in its final 10- to 12-minute cooking stage, sear and bake the fish. The Preserved Lemons are a pantry item that's either made well in advance or bought at the store.

1. Preheat the oven to 400°F. Position two racks inside the oven and/or ensure there is enough space for two large skillets to fit.

2. Place the egg whites in a large stainless-steel bowl and whisk them into a light froth. Fold in the salt until fully incorporated; the mixture should have the consistency of wet sand and be evenly moist throughout so the salt crust stays together.

3. Place the grapeseed oil in an ovenproof 10-inch skillet over high heat. Sear one of the fish in the skillet for 2 minutes on one side. Flip over the fish and sear for another 2 minutes on the other side. While the fish is searing on its second side, cover it with the salt mixture, leaving the tail end and mouth uncovered. Set the skillet aside and repeat the procedure for the second fish in a second skillet.

4. Place both skillets in the oven to bake for 10 minutes. Remove from the oven and place each whole fish, with its crust, on a serving platter. Using a large serving fork, carefully crack the crust open, keeping it as whole as possible, and remove. Cut the top filet of each fish in half lengthwise, following the outline of its backbone. Peel away the skin then lift the two halves of the top fillet off the bones, keeping them as whole as possible, and transfer to serving plates. Pick up and remove the head, tail, and bones from the bottom fillet. Cut the fillet in half lengthwise and transfer to plates. Garnish with a lemon wedge and julienned preserved lemon.

Creamed Fennel

SERVES 6 TO 8

4 fennel bulbs

2 leek stalks, white and light
green parts only, cut into
1-inch sections and soaked
in cold water (discard the
dark green tops or use for
making stock)

2 tablespoons unsalted butter

1 garlic clove, thinly sliced

pinch of red pepper flakes

½ cup dry white wine

2 cups heavy cream

¼ cup sherry vinegar

1 teaspoon fennel seeds, toasted

½ cup capers, rinsed and
drained

kosher salt and cracked
black pepper

This side dish is inspired by the creamed corn my grandmother used to make for me when I was a kid. She made it very simply, with a little onion and some pepper. I like to work with vegetables that come into season together, which explains my addition of leeks. In this recipe, the white wine, sherry vinegar, and capers achieve a nice sweet-savory balance with the cream base of the sauce.

1. Clean and wash the fennel bulbs under cold running water. Remove the cores, cut the bulbs in half, and then slice lengthwise (with the grain), about ¼ inch thick. Make sure the leeks, which had been soaking, are free of any dust or dirt.

2. Place the fennel, leeks, butter, garlic, and red pepper flakes in a large sauté pan over medium heat and cook for 8 to 10 minutes. Add the white wine and allow it to reduce by half. Add the heavy cream, vinegar, fennel seeds, capers, salt, and pepper to taste.

3. Reduce the heat to medium-low and simmer until the mixture reaches the desired consistency, 10 to 12 minutes more. This final cooking time can be increased or decreased depending on whether you prefer the sauce thicker or thinner.

Preserved Lemons

MAKES 6 WHOLE PRESERVED LEMONS

6 lemons

8 cups kosher salt

20 fresh thyme sprigs

2 cups sugar

1. Lay each lemon on its side and cut as if to quarter it but leave it whole: Make four equally spaced lengthwise cuts, to within about $\frac{1}{2}$ inch of its top and bottom. Place the lemons in a large glass or nonreactive plastic container with a tight-fitting lid and bury them in salt. Close the lid and store the container with the lemons in a cool, dry place for 10 days.

2. After 10 days, remove the lemons from the salt. Place 3 quarts water, the thyme, sugar, and 2 cups of the lemon salt in a large 5-quart stockpot. Bring the brine to a boil over high heat. Add the lemons and, when the brine comes to a boil again, turn off the heat. Allow the lemons to cool. Place them in an airtight container, cover with brine (you may not need to use all of it), and refrigerate for 2 weeks.

TO SERVE: Fully quarter the lemons, completing the partial cuts top and bottom. Place the lemons in a strainer to drain off the brine, scrape out and discard their remaining flesh, then slice and/or dice the skin as specified in a recipe or to use as a garnish.

STORAGE: The preserved lemons can be refrigerated in an airtight container for up to 6 months.

ROASTED WILD BOAR WITH SWEET POTATO PUREE, MOSTARDA, AND GRATED BITTERSWEET CHOCOLATE

SERVES 6 TO 8

1 cup olive oil

2 garlic cloves, peeled

2 tablespoons fresh rosemary
leaves

2 tablespoons kosher salt

2 teaspoons cracked black
pepper

one 8-pound rack of wild boar,
trimmed of excess fat

Sweet Potato Puree (opposite
page)

Mostarda (opposite page)

about ¼ pound (4 ounces)
bittersweet chocolate for
grating as garnish

I have a lot of fun working with recipes that not only explore the ancient origins of modern Italian cuisine but are festive and taste great. This recipe is a prime example. It has a Renaissance feel, featuring wild-game meat punctuated by garnishes of fruit compote and chocolate. Garnishing roasted pork with chocolate was quite common in places like the courts of the Medici. Wild boar roam the forests all over Europe, in many parts of Asia, and in the southern United States. Italy has its own subspecies, the population of which, with the decline of farming as an occupation in the latter half of the 20th century, actually increased. Traditional wild boar recipes include *all' agrodolce*, with *frutti di bosco*, and in various types of stews. In Tuscan and southern Italian cooking, you'll find ragù-type sauces for pasta made from wild boar meat as well as dry, cured sausages in the manner of salami, soppressata, and so forth. The meat is gamier and darker than domesticated pork.

INGREDIENT NOTE: Ask your local butcher to special-order wild boar or see Sources (page 188).

1. Preheat the oven to 400°F.

2. Place the olive oil, garlic, rosemary, salt, and pepper in a blender and puree on medium-high speed. Spread the mixture over the entire rack of boar, coating the rack well and rubbing the mixture in thoroughly. Place the meat in a roasting pan on a rack and roast for 1 hour to 1 hour and 20 minutes, or until its interior temperature reads 145–150°F on a meat thermometer.

3. Remove the rack from the oven, cover with foil, and let rest for 15 minutes. Cutting parallel to the bones, slice the rack into chops about 2 inches thick.

4. Place equal portions of the Sweet Potato Puree on each plate and top with one wild boar chop. Add a dollop of *mostarda* and/or pass it around in a serving bowl. Roughly grate about 1 tablespoon of the chocolate onto each serving of the meat.

Sweet Potato Puree

SERVES 6 TO 8

5 medium sweet potatoes,
   peeled and cut into
   ¼-inch cubes

2 cups whole milk

2 tablespoons unsalted butter

kosher salt and cracked
   black pepper

I love how this sweet potato puree balances the gaminess of the wild boar and the bitterness of the chocolate, completing a great main course for your autumn feast.

1. Place the sweet potatoes in a 5-quart heavy-bottomed saucepan, cover with water, and bring to a boil over high heat. Lower the heat to maintain a slow rolling boil and cook until the sweet potatoes are tender, about 20 minutes. Drain and return the sweet potatoes to the pan. Add the milk and butter and stir until thoroughly incorporated, 1 to 2 minutes.

2. Place the sweet potato mixture in the bowl of a food processor with the blade attachment and process for 2 to 3 minutes, until completely pureed. Season with salt and pepper.

Mostarda

SERVES 6 TO 8

1 cup dried apricots

1 cup dried pitted prunes

1 cup dried currants

1 cup dried cranberries

2 ripe pears, peeled, quartered,
   and seeded

2 cups sugar

6 cups medium-bodied red wine

1 cinnamon stick

¼ teaspoon ground cloves

There are different versions of *mostarda* served throughout Italy; my favorite is from Piemonte. *Mostarda* is often served alongside cheese, but I found it works as well or better with roasted meats.

1. Place the apricots, prunes, currants, cranberries, pears, sugar, red wine, cinnamon stick, and cloves in a 5-quart heavy-bottomed saucepan. Cover with water and bring to a boil over medium heat. Lower the heat to a simmer and cook for about 2 hours.

2. Remove the pan from the heat and allow the mixture to cool. Working in batches, place the mixture in the bowl of a food processor with the blade attachment and process for 5 to 6 minutes until pureed.

STORAGE: The mostarda can be jarred and stored in the refrigerator for up to 2 weeks

GOAT MILK PANNA COTTA WITH MACERATED CHERRIES AND GINGER BISCOTTI

SERVES 8 TO 10

4 cups goat milk

½ vanilla bean, scraped

1 cup sugar

2 cups heavy cream

6 sheets gelatin

Macerated Cherries (recipe follows)

Ginger Biscotti (page 138)

Among my favorite of the traditions we started when we opened our restaurant in Nantucket was having our own small herd of goats, taken care of by our friend Farmer Ray. At the restaurant, my right-hand man, "Bobby" (Balmoris Mendoza), made fresh goat milk cheese, ricotta, gelato, yogurt, and also this *panna cotta*, a recipe devised by Colleen, who was the pastry chef. This recipe combination, which makes for a sophisticated yet light and easy-to-prepare summer dessert, is our twist on the traditional *panna cotta* (Italian for "cooked cream") with strawberries and biscotti, typical of Emilia-Romagna's dairy heartland, where Colleen and I worked at the Picci family establishment.

Goat milk has a lot of advantages, not the least of which is its naturally tangy flavor, which I think makes it a lot more interesting than cow's milk. It also has less fat and is more easily digested, which is why it can work well for people who are lactose intolerant or allergic to cow's milk.

TIMING NOTE: The panna cotta needs an 8-hour refrigeration period. The cherries need to macerate for 24 hours, also refrigerated. The biscotti can be made well in advance.

1. Place the goat milk, vanilla bean, sugar, and heavy cream in a heavy-bottomed saucepan over low heat and bring the mixture to a lukewarm temperature. (Be sure to keep the heat quite low; overheating or scalding the goat milk can alter both its flavor and its coagulating properties.) This should take 5 to 8 minutes. Turn off the heat and, using a heat-resistant rubber spatula, stir in the gelatin sheets, one at a time, until melted and fully incorporated.

2. Prepare an ice bath. Pour the *panna cotta* mixture into a stainless-steel bowl, place the bowl in the ice bath, and stir continuously until the mixture is cooled to room temperature. Divide the mixture evenly among 8 to 10 six-ounce ramekins or custard cups (or the equivalent molds). Refrigerate for at least 8 hours, allowing the *panna cotta* to set.

3. Remove the ramekins from the fridge, top each with a generous dollop of macerated cherries, and serve chilled with the biscotti on the side.

Macerated Cherries

2 cups fresh cherries, pitted

½ cup marsala wine

COMBINE THE CHERRIES and wine in a ceramic bowl, cover with plastic wrap, and refrigerate for 24 hours.

GINGER BISCOTTI

MAKES 2 DOZEN BISCOTTI

2 cups all-purpose flour

½ cup stone-ground cornmeal

1 teaspoon baking powder

1/2 teaspoon kosher salt

4 teaspoons aniseed

1 cup sugar

3 large brown eggs, plus
   1 large yolk

1 teaspoon pure vanilla extract

½ cup grapeseed oil

zest of 1 lemon

2 tablespoons chopped fresh
   ginger

1 cup raw pistachios, coarsely
   chopped

1. Preheat the oven to 325°F.

2. Combine the flour, cornmeal, baking powder, salt, aniseed, and sugar in the bowl of an electric mixer with the paddle attachment. Beat on medium speed until all the ingredients are well incorporated, about 1 minute. Place the eggs and yolk, the vanilla, grapeseed oil, lemon zest, and ginger in a blender and puree. Pour into the bowl of the mixer and beat on medium speed until both mixtures are well incorporated and a soft, wet dough is formed, 2 to 3 minutes.

3. Line a 16 x 8-inch baking pan or baking sheet with parchment paper. Divide the dough into two equal portions. Roll each portion into an oval log about 12 inches long, 3 inches wide, and 1 inch thick. Place the logs on the baking sheet and bake until golden brown on the outside and cooked through the center, about 35 minutes. A toothpick or cake tester inserted into the center of a log should come out clean.

4. Reserving the baking sheet and parchment paper, transfer the logs to a cooling rack to cool to room temperature, about 30 minutes, then cut with a bread or other serrated-edge knife into ½-inch-thick biscotti. Lay the biscotti flat on the baking sheet, about ½ inch apart. When the baking sheet is full, place it back in the oven to bake until the biscotti are golden brown on all sides, about 10 more minutes. (Use two pans or bake in two stages if necessary.) The biscotti should be crunchy and breakable. Allow them to cool and serve at room temperature.

STORAGE: Biscotti can be stored in an airtight container at room temperature for up to 2 weeks.

~6~

CELEBRATIONS

Holidays and Special Occasions

{SERVING 10 OR MORE}

OVERLEAF: Butternut squash sformato (pages 146–147).

Holiday Tables

Here I'm intentionally not selecting a specific table for the simple reason that the Italian family creates its holiday spread wherever the special celebration takes place. The table itself is not so important but rather what everybody brings to it, starting with a strong spirit of togetherness and participation. One thing I really noticed in Italy—which again made me reflect back and gain a new appreciation of my own family growing up—was how much everybody pitched in. A lot of the ingredients would be grown on the family property. Of those that weren't, everybody brought something. They all helped out setting the table, bringing out the fancy china and serving dishes, decorating with seasonal flowers and plants, always adding special touches to signal the particular holiday or celebration.

In this chapter, I share some of the recipes I've developed for special occasions year-round. Birthdays, going-away and coming-home parties, Fourth of July, and Memorial Day—these are the usual excuses to stage a celebration for friends and family. But I don't believe in waiting for that once-a-year occasion to enjoy these recipes..

In our family, bigger celebratory gatherings were usually organized by my great-grandmother around the holidays. All our Italian relatives looked forward to these dinners with tremendous enthusiasm, anticipating great food and lots of socializing. They were all busy working people so these were their few occasions to get together and really eat and talk to their hearts' content. There was a running joke in our family about how much food wound up on the floor. Everybody was so into talking and gesturing with their hands while simultaneously attempting to chew and swallow all this delicious food, the more scraps that wound up on the floor, the better party it must have been.

Most of the recipes in this chapter come from my travels and *stages* in Italy, and some of them are tied to specific times of year. For example, the Castelluccio lentil soup recipe would be a dish Italians typically serve on New Year's Eve to help bring them prosperity. (The lentils signify coins, so the more you eat, the more fortune you are supposed to enjoy in the coming year.) If you prefer to abide strictly by tradition, wait until December 31; otherwise, recipes like this work well for a big group almost anytime. My grandmother and great-grandmother took more of the traditional approach, reserving certain dishes only for the holidays: Their *pizza **rustica*** for Christmas and New Year's comes to mind. I prefer to spread the celebratory dishes for special occasions over the entire twelve-month calendar. The pork ***spiedini***, for example, are inspired by my experience working as a chef at an ***agriturismo*** in Umbria, where we often catered weddings and other celebrations throughout the warmer months of the year.

CASTELLUCCIO LENTIL SOUP WITH RENDERED SWEET ITALIAN SAUSAGE

SERVES 10 OR MORE

1 medium carrot, cut into
1-inch pieces

1 medium Spanish onion, cut
into 1-inch cubes

2 medium celery stalks, cut into
1-inch pieces

2 tablespoons grapeseed oil

1 pound sweet Italian sausage,
casings removed

2 pounds Castelluccio lentils

2 fresh sage sprigs

8 cups water

2 tablespoons kosher salt, plus
more to taste

2 teaspoons cracked black
pepper, plus more to taste

extra virgin olive oil for garnish,
optional

Castelluccio lentils come from the town of the same name in Umbria—actually its full name is Castelluccio di Norcia—in the high plain of the Monti Sibillini, a beautiful and not very traveled area of central Italy. These specialty lentils are very small, pale brownish green in color, with a nutty taste, and they hold their shape when cooked properly. I first came across these little delights while working at the *agriturismo* Poggio dei Pettirossi in Bevagna, Umbria. (An *agriturismo* is a working farm with an inn and/or restaurant that welcomes visitors. This one had a lovely hillside of olive groves. Its name means "hill of the robin redbreasts.")

Rendering is a chef's term for cooking a food over relatively high heat so it releases at least some of its fat and becomes brown or crispy. In this recipe, the sausage is rendered in order to lend its flavors to the lentils before all the ingredients are slow-simmered into a soup.

1. Place the carrots, onions, and celery in the bowl of a food processor with the blade attachment. Process until finely chopped, 2 to 3 minutes.

2. Place the grapeseed oil in a large 5-quart saucepan over medium heat. Add the chopped vegetables and cook, stirring occasionally, until the onions are translucent, 2 to 3 minutes. Add the sausage and cook, stirring constantly, until the meat is no longer pink, 3 to 4 minutes. Add the lentils and sage and cook for 2 to 3 minutes more, stirring constantly, until the lentils are lightly toasted.

3. Add the water, raise the heat, and bring to a boil for 2 minutes. Lower the heat to maintain a steady simmer and cook for 45 minutes to 1 hour, until the lentils are tender. Add the salt and pepper and taste for seasoning, adding more if necessary. Transfer the soup to bowls, garnish each portion with about $1/2$ tablespoon extra virgin olive oil, if desired, and serve hot.

BUTTERNUT SQUASH SFORMATO

SERVES 10 OR MORE

1 large butternut squash
(2 to 3 pounds)

2 tablespoons extra virgin
olive oil

1 teaspoon kosher salt, plus
more to taste

½ teaspoon cracked black
pepper, plus more to taste

8 tablespoon (1 stick) unsalted
butter, at room temperature,
for buttering the baking pan,
plus 8 tablespoons (1 stick)
unsalted butter, melted

½ cup dried unseasoned bread
crumbs (or enough
to evenly coat the pan)

4 large brown eggs

4 large brown egg yolks

½ cup grated Parmigiano-
Reggiano

pinch of ground nutmeg

**FOR THE BÉCHAMEL SAUCE
(ABOUT 4 CUPS)**

1 pound (4 sticks) unsalted
butter

4½ cups all-purpose flour

4 quarts whole milk

1 tablespoon kosher salt, plus
more to taste

½ tablespoon cracked black
pepper, plus more to taste

Sformato is a fun Italian term, denoting a soufflé-type preparation typical of the northern regions. (Literally translated, it means something that's "unformed" or "disformed.") The consistency is custardlike—somewhere between a pudding and a soufflé. A *sformato* should be somewhat light and airy, but at the same time hearty and filling. The recipe here is meant as a side dish for a larger gathering, but it can also be served as an appetizer. Each region has its own version. The base or batter is always very similar—with butter, eggs, cheese, and béchamel—but some are made with a pie-type crust, almost like a *pizza rustica*, while others have no crust at all.

The first time I had a *sformato* was in Alba, Piemonte. There you often get multiple courses, each one topped with a shaving of white truffle, when in season. My *sformato* was made from porcini and served as an antipasto. The version offered here follows that format: The pan is buttered and lined with bread crumbs to prevent the dough from sticking, and the whole thing is placed in a water bath to bake.

TIMING NOTE: The béchamel sauce can be made while the squash is roasting in the oven. This preroasting, which takes about 40 minutes, can be done well in advance, as can the béchamel. If you have extra béchamel sauce, it can be stored in a sealed plastic container in the fridge and used for making another sformato, a fondue, or lasagna.

1. First prepare the squash: Preheat the oven to 350°F. Cut the squash in half lengthwise. Using a large kitchen spoon, scoop out the seeds and discard. Drizzle each squash half with 1 tablespoon of the extra virgin olive oil and season with ½ teaspoon of the salt and ¼ teaspoon of the pepper. Place the squash halves in a baking pan, cut side down, and cover the entire pan with aluminum foil. Roast in the oven until the squash is very tender, about 40 minutes. Remove the roasted squash halves from the oven and let cool. Once the squash is cool enough to handle, use the kitchen spoon to scoop out the flesh. This should yield 3 cups of squash. Discard the skin, place the roasted squash in a food processor with the metal blade, and puree until smooth. Season with salt and pepper and set aside.

2. While the squash is roasting, make the béchamel sauce: Place the butter in a 5-quart heavy-bottomed saucepan over very low heat. Once the butter is melted, whisk in the flour. Continue whisking until all the flour has been absorbed and a wet, pasty roux forms. Continue cooking on low heat for several minutes until the roux is pale golden brown in color and has a nutty aroma.

3. While whisking, begin slowly adding the milk, making sure the mixture is completely smooth and lump free. Continue to cook over low heat for another 10 minutes, adding the first 2 quarts of milk 2 cups at a time, and the second 2 quarts all at once. The roux and the milk should be completely incorporated into

a fondue-like mixture; it should have some resistance and form a slight ribbon when a spoon is passed through it. Season the béchamel liberally with the salt and pepper, adding more if necessary. Pass the bèchamel through a strainer or chinois into a stainless-steel bowl and let cool to room temperature, stirring occasionally with a heat-resistant rubber spatula. Set aside.

4. Increase the oven to 400°F. Butter a 9 x 11 x 3-inch baking pan. Add the bread crumbs to the pan and toss well so the entire inside of the pan is evenly coated. Discard any loose bread crumbs.

5. Combine the 3 cups pureed squash, 4 cups béchamel sauce, melted butter, eggs, egg yolks, Parmigiano-Reggiano, and nutmeg in a large bowl. Whisk until completely incorporated.

6. Pour the mixture into the breaded baking pan. Cover with aluminum foil and place in a larger pan with warm water coming roughly halfway up the sides of the *sformato* pan. Place the entire water bath in the oven to bake for 35 to 40 minutes, until the center of the *sformato* is just set. It should be the consistency of a firm pudding.

7. Remove the foil from the pan and bake an additional 5 minutes to color the top of the *sformato*. Let rest on a cooling rack for 10 minutes, scoop out portions with a serving spoon, and serve warm or at room temperature.

CARAMELIZED BRUSSELS SPROUTS WITH CRISPY GUANCIALE

SERVES 10 OR MORE

3 pounds Brussels sprouts

2 tablespoons grapeseed oil

½ medium Spanish onion, finely diced (⅛-inch cubes)

½ pound guanciale, cut into ½-inch cubes

about 1 teaspoon kosher salt, plus more for blanching and seasoning

about ¼ teaspoon cracked black pepper, plus more to taste

Most Italians insist that dishes like spaghetti alla carbonara and bucatini all'Amatriciana cannot be reproduced without the use of guanciale. Substitute pancetta if you must, but don't claim the dish is authentic. In this tasty side dish, I find the unique qualities of the guanciale to be the perfect match for Brussels sprouts. The meat comes from the pork cheek or jowl (*guancia* means "cheek"). Traditionally, it is rubbed in spices, wrapped in burlap, and cured inside a mountain cave (as opposed to being smoked) for six months before being air-dried. The result is quite distinct from bacon or pancetta, with a smoother, more luscious texture and more sophisticated flavor. I think of Brussels sprouts as a fall or winter vegetable and almost always serve this recipe alongside the turkey at family Thanksgiving dinners. It also works well with chicken or pork.

1. Wash and drain the Brussels sprouts. Remove their tough outer leaves and cut off and discard their hard stems. Bring a very large pot of water containing a small handful of salt (about 1½ tablespoons) to a boil over high heat. Place the Brussels sprouts in the water, turn off the heat, and allow them to blanch for 2 minutes. Drain the Brussels sprouts under cold running water for 1 to 2 minutes.

2. Place the grapeseed oil a large 12-inch sauté pan with over medium heat. Add the onions and guanciale. Cook, stirring occasionally, until the onions are translucent and the guanciale is brown around the edges and crisp.

3. Add the Brussels sprouts and continue to cook over medium heat for 3 to 4 minutes, stirring constantly to make sure they don't stick to the bottom of the pan. Season with the salt and pepper; adjust the seasonings. Transfer to a large platter and serve hot.

GRILLED PORK SPIEDINI WITH FRESH PLUMS, SAUSAGE, AND ROSEMARY

SERVES 10 OR MORE

4 pounds pork tenderloin, cut
into 2-inch cubes

1 pound ripe plums, cut into
½-inch wedges

2 pounds sweet Italian sausage,
cut into 1-inch segments

½ cup olive oil for brushing and
drizzling, optional

3 fresh rosemary sprigs,
leaves only

2 tablespoons kosher salt

2 teaspoons cracked black
pepper

Of course I had seen skewers before, but never as many as at the *agriturismo* in Umbria where I worked for a summer. *Spiedini* is the Italian word for both the skewers themselves and also the dishes prepared by alternating pieces of meat or fish and vegetables on those skewers and grilling them quickly over a hot fire. Over the course of the summer, I saw the proprietor Marco grill literally thousands of bits of meat—sausages, pork, veal—over an open flame. We often catered weddings on the property and *spiedini* were a staple of those celebrations. My variation involves adding plums, a quintessentially summery fruit.

TIMING NOTE: The wooden skewers need to be soaked in water for 24 hours in advance.

1. Submerge about two dozen wooden or bamboo skewers in water and soak for 24 hours.

2. Prepare an outdoor grill with a high heat source. Position the rack 6 to 8 inches from the fire or flame.

3. Skewer the pieces of pork, plum, and sausage, alternating in that order, until all the skewers are filled. Brush the full skewers with olive oil, and season with the rosemary, salt, and pepper.

4. Brush the grill rack lightly with olive oil. Position the skewers on the rack with at least ½ inch of space between them and cook until evenly done all over, 3 to 4 minutes per side. Use tongs to transfer the skewers to a large platter, garnish with a drizzle of extra virgin olive oil, if desired, and serve.

SEAFOOD SAFFRON RISOTTO WITH ENGLISH PEAS AND GRATED RICOTTA SALATA

SERVES 10 OR MORE

2 pounds medium bearded (wild) mussels

2 tablespoons grapeseed oil

1 cup chopped Spanish onions

1 teaspoon (loosely packed) saffron

2 cups Carnaroli rice

1 cup fresh English peas

½ cup dry white wine

6 cups water

kosher salt and cracked black pepper

5 tablespoons unsalted butter

½ cup grated Parmigiano-Reggiano cheese

1 garlic clove, sliced

pinch of red pepper flakes

2 pounds medium sea scallops, dry and cut in quarters

1 pound medium shrimp, peeled and deveined

1 cup grated ricotta salata

In my previous book, I outlined my approach to risotto, which includes the use of water as the cooking liquid and also the presentation of the flavoring ingredients as a topping rather than mixed in with the rice. I've found that a protein-based stock tends to break down the structure of the individual grains much more readily, which means the grains release their starch more quickly and turn the risotto mushy rather than allowing it to retain its nice toothsome mouth feel. To serve, I like to mound the risotto on the plate or platter and then place the "sauce" in the middle on top, a traditional way of serving many pasta dishes. I'm very partial to this idea of presenting the two main components of the dish as separate and discreet: It allows diners to taste and judge both of them for their respective merits and then combine them on the plate at will. Perhaps most important, a lot of flavor ingredients (particularly seafood) tend to get rubbery and overdone if they're mixed in with the rice during the cooking process; I've found that is the best way to avoid that pitfall.

Peas are a classic spring and early summer vegetable: We always obtain them as fresh and local as possible and shuck them by hand at the restaurants. Fresh ones are far preferable for this recipe, but high-quality frozen peas can be used during the off-season. Since they contain extra moisture, though, they should be added much later, along with the butter and Parmigiano-Reggiano; you should also cook the rice an additional minute or so at the end to evaporate that extra water.

INGREDIENT NOTES: Wild mussels—the ones with the beards—are far preferable; for me, the best ones are from the cold, clear waters of Maine. Medium shrimp and medium sea scallops are called for; if you can get genuine Nantucket bay scallops, when in season (October to November), they are a treat not to be missed. With the grated ricotta salata in this recipe, we're violating the famous age-old Italian taboo of serving no cheese with seafood. Of course, it's true that most cheeses, which are pungent, just don't work with seafood; they overwhelm its fresh, subtle flavors. The ricotta salata, however, is a salty cheese that goes happily hand in hand with seafood—two salty yet balanced ingredients that find harmony together.

TIMING NOTE: The mussels are best when soaked in advance so they filter out any internal grit. Begin preparing the topping at the third stage of cooking the risotto, that is, as you are adding the third 2-cup measure of water.

1. Place the mussels in a large bowl or pot of cold salted water for 1 to 2 hours. Drain the water, pull the beards off the mussels, and rinse the mussels thoroughly under cold running water while rubbing or brushing their shells.

2. Place the grapeseed oil, onions, and saffron in a 3-quart saucepan. Sauté over medium heat, stirring occasionally with a wooden spoon, until translucent, 3 to 4 minutes. The onions should not take on any color; lower the heat if necessary.

3. Stir the rice into the onions and toast for 1 to 2 minutes, until the rice dries out and the kernels become opaque. Add the peas and shake the pan occasionally to keep the rice from sticking to the bottom. Add the white wine and let it evaporate. Begin to add the water 2 cups at a time, continuing to stir the rice as it releases its starch, and occasionally shaking the pan to prevent sticking. (The water will be added in three stages.) Drag the spoon through the rice, and when the rice is thick enough to reveal a pathway, add the next 2 cups of water and repeat the procedure. Add 1 teaspoon salt and $\frac{1}{4}$ teaspoon pepper. After adding the last 2 cups of water to the rice, add 3 tablespoons of the butter and the Parmigiano-Reggiano, and stir until fully melted and incorporated. Adjust the seasonings.

4. While the risotto is absorbing its last addition of water, place the remaining 2 tablespoons butter, the garlic, and red pepper flakes in a 10-inch skillet over medium heat. When the butter is melted, add the mussels, scallops, and shrimp. Cook until the butter is lightly browned, the mussels open up, and the scallops and shrimp are cooked through, shaking the pan occasionally to avoid sticking, 5 to 6 minutes. (Discard any unopened mussels.)

5. Mound the risotto on a large platter and place the seafood topping in the center. Garnish with the grated ricotta salata

TURNIP GRATIN WITH CRUSHED AMARETTI

SERVES 10 OR MORE

1 tablespoon unsalted butter
for greasing

6 large white turnips, peeled and
sliced ¼ inch thick

2 tablespoons kosher salt

2 teaspoons cracked black
pepper

4 cups heavy cream

1 cup grated Parmigiano-
Reggiano

6 packages amaretti
(12 cookies), crushed

Ever since I was a kid, scalloped potatoes have been one of my favorite side dishes. Turnips, also a root vegetable, are intrinsically much more interesting than potatoes. So when I was creating menus for my restaurants, inspired by my love for that potato dish, I came up with this recipe. I "Italianized" it with Parmigiano-Reggiano cheese and added a garnish of crushed amaretti. Turnips are slightly bitter, so adding the sweetness of the amaretti and the nutty flavor of the Parmigiano-Reggiano made a lot of sense.

INGREDIENT NOTE: If you bite into an *amaretto* cookie, its flavor, with bittersweet almond and sugar components, can be pretty assertive. But little bits of crushed ones, sprinkled in with grated Parmigiano-Reggiano and layered throughout a smooth, creamy baked casserole create a nice balance and contrast. When I call for crushed *amaretti*, I'm assuming the cookies will be in their hard, crunchy state, which they attain after they've been stored in their metal tin for a few days. Most of those you get in the store will already be hard enough to crumble into crushed bits.

1. Preheat the oven to 400°F. Lightly grease a large 13 x 9-inch ovenproof glass baking dish with the butter.

2. Line the bottom of the baking dish with a layer of turnip slices. The slices should be slightly overlapping to cover the entire bottom of the dish. Season with a pinch of salt and a pinch of pepper. Pour 1 cup of the heavy cream on this first layer, spreading it evenly. Sprinkle with 4 tablespoons of the Parmigiano-Reggiano and a third of the crushed amaretti, spreading them both evenly. Repeat with a second layer of turnip slices, a pinch of salt, pinch of pepper, 1 cup of the heavy cream, 4 more tablespoons of the Parmigiano-Reggiano, and a third of the crushed amaretti. Repeat with an identical third layer, finishing the top with the remainder of the Parmigiano-Reggiano and amaretti. .

3. Cover the baking dish with aluminum foil, place on a baking sheet, and bake until the turnips are fork tender, 45 minutes to 1 hour. Remove the foil and bake for 10 minutes more, until the top is lightly browned. Remove from the oven, let cool for 6 to 8 minutes, and serve.

POACHED SAUSAGE AND ONIONS IN BAGNA CAUDA

SERVES 10 OR MORE

4 cups olive oil

4 salt-cured anchovy fillets,
   rinsed and patted dry

5 pounds sweet Italian sausages

1 medium Spanish onion, sliced
   into 2-inch wedges

1 tablespoon red pepper flakes

kosher salt and cracked
   black pepper

Bagna cauda is a classic dipping sauce originally from northern Italy. The phrase itself, in Piemontese, translates to "hot bath." The dip is olive oil–based and usually contains garlic, anchovies, perhaps some red pepper flakes, and parsley. Most chefs have their own variations, many of which also include melted butter or even cream. The bagna cauda is served with an assortment of raw vegetables as an appetizer, buffet platter, or light lunch—the Italian version of crudités.

The traditional *bagna cauda* inspired me to cook these sausage in a "hot bath" of olive oil, so I borrowed the name for the recipe title as well. You can save the sausage's cooking oil and reuse it in a number of ways, including for classic bagna cauda. Poaching has always been one of my favorite methods for cooking fish (see Olive Oil–Poached Fluke, page 108) and it also works well for sausage. First and foremost, when you cook sausages fast over high heat, their casing bursts and all the juices come out. In Germany and Eastern Europe, where bratwurst and many other forms of sausage originated, they always poach them. This way, you get sausage that is moist on the inside and highlights its own flavors, rather than those from browning or caramelizing the outside. The anchovies work as a flavor enhancer, adding salty seasoning.

1. Preheat the oven to 400°F.

2. Place the olive oil, anchovy fillets, sausages, and onions in a large 13 x 9-inch ovenproof glass or ceramic baking dish or casserole, making sure the sausages are completely submerged in the olive oil. (Use two casseroles and divide equal portions of the ingredients between them if necessary.) Place the casserole in the oven for 45 minutes, or until the sausages and onions are completely cooked. The onions should be translucent, and the sausages should take on a light brown color.

3. Remove the casserole from the oven and season the sausages with salt and pepper. Transfer to a large platter with some of the onions and a small amount of the olive oil, and serve hot.

STORAGE: The leftover olive oil can be stored in a covered glass or ceramic container in the refrigerator for up to 2 weeks and reused to poach other vegetables or meats.

SICILIAN WINE CRACKERS WITH PLUM JAM AND ASSORTED CHEESES

MAKES ABOUT 2 DOZEN CRACKERS

1 cup all-purpose flour

1 cup whole wheat flour

8 tablespoons sugar

2 teaspoons ground fennel seed

2 teaspoons kosher salt

1 teaspoon cracked black pepper

½ cup dry red wine

½ cup extra virgin olive oil

about 1 tablespoon raw cane sugar, for sprinkling

Colleen's grandfather, Joe Piazza, emigrated from Sicily with his parents as a young boy. They were from Termini Imerese, just outside Palermo. During World War II, Joe was stationed in Naples, which perhaps explains why his lifelong business was named the Café di Napoli. This is a genuine Sicilian recipe—from Joe's family—that's great for special occasions or holidays. It's easy to make, with all the ingredients combined in one bowl, and can be prepared well in advance.

These wine crackers have a consistency somewhere between a biscuit and a cracker, with a good deal of crunch. Their flavor is both savory and a little sweet so they work particularly well as part of a dessert cheese course, which is how we served them at our restaurants: alongside a selection of three or four fine Italian cheeses. Try a genuine two- or three-year-old DOP Parmigiano-Reggiano, an aged pecorino di Pienza, Taleggio, and Gorgonzola. Some of these cheeses are quite pungent and salty, which is where the Plum Jam (see opposite page) comes in—to provide a smooth, sweet counterbalance. If you keep your cheeses in the fridge, they are best served if you take them out about an hour in advance.

1. Preheat the oven to 350°F.

2. Place the all-purpose flour, whole wheat flour, sugar, fennel, salt, pepper, red wine, and olive oil in a medium stainless-steel bowl. Combine them by hand until they are well incorporated into a malleable, somewhat oily mixture the consistency of Play-Doh. Set aside to rest for 30 minutes at room temperature.

3. Cut two sheets of parchment paper 12 x 24 inches (to fit a baking sheet or cookie sheet of that size). Flatten the ball of dough between the two pieces of paper, then roll it out with a rolling pin to a very thin thickness of ⅛ inch or less. Place the rolled-out cookie dough, with parchment paper top and bottom, on a 12 x 24-inch baking sheet. Bake for 20 minutes, until the dough attains a slight golden color. Remove the sheet from the oven and peel off and discard the top layer of parchment paper.

4. Using a handheld crinkle pasta or cookie cutter, cut the baked dough into diamond-shaped sections, 1 inch on each side and 2 inches from top to bottom. Leave the baked dough on the sheet, sprinkle it with cane sugar, and place it back in the oven to bake for another 5 to 6 minutes.

5. Remove the sheet from the oven and let the baked, unseparated crackers cool. When cool enough to handle, break the crackers along their crinkle-cut edges.

STORAGE: The crackers can be stored in a sealed airtight container at room temperature for up to 2 weeks.

Plum Jam

MAKES ABOUT 6 QUARTS

1 cinnamon stick

1 vanilla bean

1 teaspoon ground cloves

1 tablespoon cracked black
pepper

1 tablespoon aniseed

1 teaspoon ground nutmeg

5 pieces cardamon

5 pounds plums, quartered,
pitted, skin left on

two 750 milliliter bottles dry
red wine

12½ cups water

4 cups sugar

2 cups golden raisins

2 cups dried figs

2 cups dried pitted prunes

2 medium navel oranges, cut into
½-inch thick slices

kosher salt

This jam is my own Suhanosky family recipe. It's sweet but not super-sweet; it maintains a good component of acidity, which makes it great to serve alongside those aforementioned cheeses, as well as roasted meats and even as a dab on top of chicken liver crostini. Peaches, apricots, cherries, strawberries—whatever's fresh and in season—can be substituted for the plums, but I recommend you keep the dried fruits and quantities the same.

1. Place the cinnamon stick, vanilla bean, cloves, pepper, aniseed, nutmeg, and cardamom in a cast-iron skillet over medium heat. Using a wooden spoon to fold over and combine them, toast until aromatic, 6 to 8 minutes.

2. Place the toasted spices, plums, red wine, water, sugar, raisins, figs, prunes, and oranges in a large 5-quart, heavy-bottomed stockpot. Bring to a boil, cover, reduce the heat to low, and cook down to a desired consistency, at least 2 hours and up to 5. (If you like your jam really thick, cook it for closer to 5 hours; if less thick, closer to 2 hours.)

3. Stir the jam occasionally and thin it with water to adjust the consistency as needed. Taste after 2 hours and add up to 1 tablespoon salt if necessary. When the jam is done, remove the vanilla bean and cinnamon stick and pass it through a food mill. Let cool to room temperature.

STORAGE: The jam can be canned or jarred for up to 2 months in the pantry or put in airtight containers in the fridge for up to 2 weeks. If refrigerated, bring to room temperature before serving.

COLLEEN'S LEMON BERRY TART

MAKES 1 TART (ABOUT 10 SERVINGS)

FOR THE TART DOUGH

½ pound (about 1½ cups)
   all-purpose flour, plus more
   for flouring

1 tablespoon sugar

1 teaspoon kosher salt

12 tablespoons (1½ sticks)
   chilled unsalted butter, cut
   into ½-inch cubes (note: the
   first 1¼ sticks are for the tart
   dough, the last ¼ stick is for
   dotting the tart before baking)

⅓ cup ice water

juice of ¼ lemon

stone-ground cornmeal for
   dusting

Gelato (page 40)

FOR THE LEMON CURD

3 large brown eggs

½ cup sugar

½ cup freshly squeezed lemon
   juice

zest of 1 lemon

½ teaspoon kosher salt

4 tablespoons (½ stick) unsalted
   butter, chilled and cut into
   ½-inch cubes

A rustic fruit *torta* at the end of a celebratory meal is something you'll find in most Italian households. Tarts are an elegant simple way to highlight delicious seasonal fruits, profiling their wonderful fresh flavors. Colleen has mastered a perfectly flaky crust, which is included in this recipe. It can hold any seasonal fruit desired: She's made it with only blueberries but here it has an assortment of berries including strawberries, blackberries, raspberries, and blueberries, all of which work fine as long as you cut the larger ones down to the same size as the smaller. It can also be made with poached apples or pears, or oven-roasted stone fruits. (Always remember to save the poaching liquid: Reduced, it makes a perfect sauce for the final presentation.) When we served these tarts in the restaurant, Colleen would top them with a generous scoop of homemade gelato, adding a decadent flourish. It's a great way to finish a special family-style meal without overdoing it.

TIMING NOTE: The tart dough requires a minimum of 4 hours chilling time; it can also be chilled overnight in advance. The entire tart can be made ahead of time and frozen so you can put it in the oven while having dinner and it will be ready to serve warm at the end of the meal. The lemon curd can also be made well in advance.

1. First make the dough: Place the flour, sugar, and salt in the bowl of a food processor with the blade attachment, and pulse once to mix the ingredients. Lay 10 tablespoons (1¼ stick) of the butter cubes, evenly spaced, on top of the flour. Pulse 10 times or until the butter is roughly combined into the flour mixture. It should retain a coarse texture and there should still be some whole chunks of butter to ensure the flakiness of the final baked product. Lightly flour a work surface about 2 feet square. Combine the ice water and lemon juice, then slowly pour the mixture into the food processor, pulsing about five times until the dough just comes together. Once the dough begins to form a single mass, transfer it to the floured work surface.

2. With the palms of your hands, flatten the dough out in three directions. You should push it flat just one time, making sure to smear any large chunks of butter, leaving them in streaks. Scrape the dough back up with your hands and form it into a ball. Flatten the dough ball into a disk about ½ inch thick. Wrap the disk tightly in plastic wrap and chill in the refrigerator for at least 4 hours or overnight.

3. To make the lemon curd, place the eggs, sugar, lemon juice, lemon zest, and salt in a medium saucepan over low heat. Whisk until the mixture thickens to a pudding consistency, about 8 minutes. Remove from the heat and pass through a wire mesh strainer into a bowl. While the mixture is still hot, stir in the butter with a rubber spatula and continue to stir as it cools, about 5 minutes. If not using right

FOR THE BERRIES

3 cups mixed berries (such as
    blueberries, strawberries,
    and raspberries), cut to
    the same size

¼ cup sugar

zest of 1 lemon

1 teaspoon ground cinnamon

away, place the lemon curd in an airtight container and store in the refrigerator for up to 5 days.

4. For the berry mixture, place the berries, sugar, lemon zest, and cinnamon in a large stainless-steel bowl, toss to combine, and set aside at room temperature for 15 minutes.

5. Preheat the oven to 400°F. Remove the dough disk from the refrigerator about 30 minutes in advance; it should come to room temperature.

6. Lightly flour a work surface. Flour the dough disk then shake off any excess. Place it on the work surface and, using a rolling pin, gradually roll it out to a thickness of ¼ inch, rotating one quarter turn counterclockwise after each pass of the rolling pin. The dough should form an 8-inch circle.

7. Spread the lemon curd to a thickness of about ½ inch on top of the center of the tart dough, leaving a 2-inch border around the edges. Pour the berries on top of the lemon curd. Dot the filling with the remaining ½ stick of cubed butter. Fold the sides of the dough up to form the tart, making sure the berries are gathered and contained within. Chill the tart in the refrigerator for at least 30 minutes. Alternatively, it can be wrapped in plastic and placed in an airtight container in the freezer for up to 2 days.

8. Dust a 9 x 13-inch baking sheet with cornmeal. Place the tart on the baking sheet and bake for 30 minutes. Rotate the tart and bake for 15 minutes more or until the berries are bubbly and the crust golden brown. Serve hot with gelato on the side.

~7~

ALFRESCO

Taking It Outdoors

{SERVING 18 TO 20}

OVERLEAF: Soft-shell crab sandwiches with watercress, aioli, and fingerling potato salad (pages 177–178).

The Cape House Table

This book is about sharing my connection to the communal eating culture of Italy, first through my family's Italian-American roots and then through the inspiration I picked up in the old country itself. The connection is never stronger than when it comes to large fair-weather feasts. Almost every house I saw in southern Italy had a terrace or patio, with a grill or wood oven. We traveled throughout Calabria and Sicily, visiting family and friends in places like Tropea, the onion capital, where outdoor living and dining is such a part of the lifestyle. We visited Colleen's relatives in Termini Erminise outside Palermo. I remember it was March and really pleasant out, with just a slight chill in the air at night. We went to Salina, in the Aeolian islands, where they filmed "Il Postino," and enjoyed more of the same. Coming home inspired, we recreated the feeling during summers in Nantucket and on the Cape.

Every summer, my sister-in-law, Jen Hawkins, and her husband, Tom, invite us to his family's beach house, which sits on a secluded 13-acre property on Cape Cod, by the shores of Buzzard's Bay. We thoroughly enjoy our family time at the "Cape House," where among the highlights are our large family meals. We gather on the porch around the big old wooden table, and the spotlight is on the simple, classic Italian-inspired summer dishes we love so much. Tom brings his love of fishing, Jen her keen eye for setting the scene, and Colleen and I our vocation for food. With ready access to fresh fish and local produce, and everybody working together, it feels so easy to create many delicious and memorable meals. Whether it's a lazy lunch stretching well into the afternoon or a leisurely dinner while enjoying the sunset, these outdoor meals at the Cape House table represent a special time of year and hold a very special place in our hearts.

To me, there is nothing better than dining *alfresco*. It is absolutely magical. Not to mention all the beautiful fresh seasonal produce I think of as earmarked for these occasions, starting with perfectly ripe local tomatoes and juicy peaches and plums. Along with those, all you need are a few simple recipes, an outdoor table, and the guests to fill the seats. Whatever the time of year, whenever I taste a Caprese salad or a dish of grilled meat, I start to dream about those wonderful outdoor gatherings in the dog days of summer, featuring a lively crowd, simple preparations, and the smell of the grill wafting out across the dunes. Living as I do on the East Coast, I start to think about outdoor dining beginning in early May and try to extend it well into October. For those of us who endure cold winters, this chapter is full of much-anticipated warm-weather treats. For those who live in a year-round summer climate, you're in luck, because you can put this chapter to work for you twelve months of the year. The recipes are designed for large gatherings of eighteen to twenty, or more, in a picnic-type setting.

SLICED NATIVE TOMATOES, WATERMELON, BUFFALO MOZZARELLA, AND PESTO

SERVES 18 TO 20

2 cups olive oil, plus
    3 tablespoons for garnish

1 garlic clove

2½ cups pine nuts, toasted

2 cups (tightly packed) fresh
    basil leaves

1 teaspoon kosher salt, plus
    more to taste

¼ teaspoon cracked black
    pepper, plus more to taste

8 medium beefsteak tomatoes
    (5 pounds), cored and cut
    into slices ½ inch thick and
    2 to 2½ inches in diameter

3 pounds seedless watermelon,
    sliced into triangles
    ¼ inch thick and 2 to
    2½ inches wide

eight 8-ounce balls buffalo
    mozzarella (4 pounds), cut
    into slices ½ inch thick and
    2 to 2½ inches in diameter

This is a very summery dish, mouthwatering on a hot day, visually appealing, and lending itself perfectly to larger special-occasion gatherings. More than ten years ago, before it became the universal "new" Caprese salad, I was offering sliced native tomatoes with watermelon and buffalo mozzarella as an antipasto on my summer menus in Nantucket and New York. Adding watermelon to this classic combination makes the salad fresher and lighter; the pesto gives it added zest.

INGREDIENT NOTE: Buffalo mozzarella is top-quality fresh mozzarella made from the milk of domesticated water buffaloes. The milk is thick and rich and particularly well suited for making this type of cheese. The genuine article (mozzarella di bufala) comes from specially designated regions in the vicinity of Naples; there are also well-made "imitations" from other parts of Italy and also the United States. I like to buy the medium balls (about 8 ounces each), which are convenient to slice into rounds roughly the same size as a slice of a medium tomato. If those aren't available, you can just start from the standard one-pound portions. The tomatoes for this salad should be juicy ripe and preferably fresh from a local farm.

1. Place the 2 cups olive oil, the garlic, and pine nuts in a blender and blend at medium speed until the ingredients are the consistency of a somewhat rough-textured paste, 2 to 3 minutes. Add the basil, salt, and pepper. Blend at medium speed until the basil is fully incorporated into the oil paste and the pesto is a uniform consistency, 2 to 3 minutes more.

2. Arrange the slices of tomatoes, watermelon, and mozzarella, alternating in that order, to cover an entire large platter in one layer. The slices should overlap so that half of each one is showing. Season the entire platter with a couple generous pinches of salt and pepper.

3. Use a large kitchen spoon to drizzle the pesto evenly over all the slices. Garnish with olive oil and serve. Note: If necessary, repeat the process of arranging, seasoning, and dressing the slices, creating a second layer on top of the first. (Or, if you prefer, use a second platter.)

CHILLED ZUCCHINI SOUP WITH SAUSAGE AND MINT

SERVES 18 TO 20

1 large carrot, cut into 1-inch pieces

1 medium Spanish onion, cut into 1-inch cubes

2 medium celery stalks, cut into 1-inch pieces

3 tablespoons grapeseed oil

5 pounds zucchini, stems removed, cut into 2-inch cubes

8 ounces mascarpone

2 teaspoons kosher salt

1 teaspoon cracked black pepper

2 pounds sweet Italian sausages, removed from the casings

1 cup (tightly packed) fresh mint leaves

It would be difficult to imagine another dish that speaks more of summer than a chilled zucchini soup. Zucchini grow likes weeds during the warm season. For those of you scratching your heads about what to do with such abundance, here is an excellent solution. Its pureed base is smooth, fresh, and light. It's enriched with some mascarpone, chilled, garnished with refreshing mint, and finally "Italianized" with a dollop of sausage. (If you prefer to go a lighter, vegetarian route, simply skip the sausage step.)

TIMING NOTE: The soup has a chilling period of 3 hours in the fridge.

1. Place the carrots, onions, and celery in the bowl of a food processor with the blade attachment and process until finely chopped.

2. Place 2 tablespoons of the grapeseed oil in a large 5-quart saucepan over medium heat. Add the chopped vegetables, and cook until the onions are translucent, 2 to 3 minutes. Add the zucchini cubes and continue to cook, stirring occasionally, for 3 to 4 minutes more. Add enough water to cover the zucchini (about 4 cups), raise the heat, and bring to a boil for 2 to 3 minutes. Lower the heat to maintain a simmer and cook for 20 minutes more.

3. Whisk in the mascarpone until completely melted and incorporated, and remove the pan from the heat.

4. In stages, transfer the zucchini mixture to a blender and blend on medium speed for 2 to 3 minutes, or until fully pureed. Stir in the salt and pepper. Transfer the pureed soup to a nonreactive container and place in the refrigerator to chill for 3 hours.

5. Place the remaining 1 tablespoon grapeseed oil in a 10-inch skillet over medium heat. Add the sausage meat and cook, stirring regularly, until it has taken on a light brown color, 3 to 4 minutes. Discard the excess fat from the pan and set the sausage aside to cool to room temperature.

6. Julienne the mint leaves by cutting them into $1/4$-inch-thick strips. Place about 1 cup of soup in each serving bowl, then garnish with 1 heaping tablespoon sausage and 1 tablespoon julienned mint.

PUNTARELLE IN CAESAR DRESSING

SERVES 18 TO 20

3 heads puntarelle, cut into
¼-inch strips

6 large brown egg yolks

2 garlic cloves

4 anchovy fillets, patted dry

¼ cup fresh lemon juice

1 cup grapeseed oil

½ cup grated Parmigiano-
Reggiano

1 tablespoon kosher salt, plus
more to taste

2 teaspoons cracked black
pepper, plus more to taste

1 cup unseasoned bread
crumbs, toasted

Puntarelle are a variety of chicory, with serrated leaves somewhat like dandelion greens. The name itself is Roman for "little points" or "little pointy things." They are considered the quintessential Roman vegetable, perhaps second only to artichokes. Flavorwise, puntarelle offer hints of endive, perhaps fennel, and are slightly bitter like other types of chicory. They stand up very nicely to a strong dressing like this Caesar one, with its hearty helping of anchovies. To make a salad, puntarelle are traditionally first soaked in ice water so they curl up into a friséelike shape and become juicier and less bitter. Chicory, which may be more readily available, can be substituted. It, too, should be soaked in ice water in advance.

TIMING NOTE: The *puntarelle* are soaked for 3 hours in advance.

1. Place the puntarelle in a bath of ice water for 3 hours, or until they have curled up. Place the curled puntarelle in a large strainer or colander and drain for 30 minutes.

2. Meanwhile, place the egg yolks, garlic, and anchovy fillets in a blender and blend at low speed for 2 minutes. Add the lemon juice and continue to blend on low speed while slowly pouring in the grapeseed oil in a steady stream until it is evenly incorporated. Adjust the mixture to a creamy consistency by adding water, 1 tablespoon at a time, if necessary. Add the Parmigiano-Reggiano and blend on low speed until the cheese is fully incorporated, about 2 minutes more. Add the salt and pepper, then turn off the blender.

3. Place the Caesar dressing in a large stainless-steel bowl. Add the puntarelle and toss until the dressing evenly coats all the curlicues, about 2 minutes. Transfer to a large platter and garnish with a sprinkling of bread crumbs.

LINGUINE WITH CLAMS OREGANATA AND PANCETTA

SERVES 18 TO 20

5 pounds littleneck clams (shells 1 to 2 inches in diameter)

4 tablespoons grapeseed oil

1 pound pancetta, diced into ¼-inch cubes)

4 tablespoons kosher salt

1 cup tightly packed fresh oregano leaves

2 garlic cloves, thinly sliced

¼ teaspoon red pepper flakes

2 cups dry white cooking wine

4 pounds linguine

2 cups fresh bread crumbs, toasted

My favorite pasta dishes are often based on seafood—7 of the 18 recipes for fresh pasta in my first book, for example, featured seafood—and of course linguine with white clam sauce is the mother of all such recipes. Clams oreganata, on the other hand, is a universally beloved Italian-American dish of stuffed clams that highlights fresh oregano and bread crumbs. I combined the two and turned it into this simple recipe that yields a big bowl of pasta, ideal for sharing at large parties during the warm summer months. I always think of using freshly dug littlenecks off the coast of Buzzard's Bay.

INGREDIENT NOTES: Littlenecks are the smaller classification of the hard-shell clams native to the East Coast of the United States. Also known by their Indian name, "quahog," these delicious bivalve mollusks should be bought and consumed as local and as fresh as possible. The smaller the clams, the sweeter and more tender their meat. Littlenecks are generally defined as having shells less than 2 inches across; cherrystones are a bit larger (about 2½ inches in diameter); and chowder clams larger still, up to 3½ inches. Regarding the dry pasta, I like a traditionally manufactured artisanal type—among my favorite brands is Setaro, from Torre Annunziata, near Naples—which is extruded through bronze dies. It's a thicker cut, with a bit rougher surface. It is less brittle, doesn't dry so hard and crack so easily, as more commercial brands do, and it also releases a good deal of its starch when cooked so the cooking water can be used to emulsify the sauce, which in turn will mix with and coat the pasta better.

TIMING NOTE: To remove any grit and clean the clams well, it's best to soak them in cold water for at least 1 hour in advance and then rinse them thoroughly (see step 1). In extensive testing of dry pasta recipes, I've found that the manufacturers' instructions on the packages generally recommend about 2 minutes excessive cooking time. In other words, if you want your pasta cooked perfectly al dente, start tasting it at least 2 minutes short of the stated time and remember that it will continue to cook after you remove it from its water and mix it with the sauce.

1. To prepare the clams, place them in a large bowl or pot of cold salted water for 1 to 2 hours. Discard the water and rinse the clams thoroughly under cold running water while rubbing or brushing their shells.

2. Place the grapeseed oil in a large 5-quart stockpot over medium heat. Add the clams and the pancetta, cover the pot, and cook, stirring occasionally, for 8 to 10 minutes or until the pancetta is crispy and has released its fat, and the clams have all opened. (Discard any unopened clams.)

3. While the clams and pancetta are cooking, fill two 5-quart pots two-thirds full of water, add 2 tablespoons of salt to each pot, place them over high heat and bring the water to a boil.

4. Add the oregano, garlic, and red pepper flakes to the clams and pancetta, stir well to combine, and cook for 1 more minute.

5. Add 2 pounds linguine to each pot of boiling water and stir constantly for 2 minutes. Continue to cook until the pasta is al dente (slightly chewy or toothsome); see timing note above.

6. Add the white wine to the clams and cook, still over medium heat, until reduced by half, about 1 minute. Add $1^{1}/_{2}$ cups of the linguine cooking water and cook, again until reduced by half, about 2 minutes more.

7. Using a wire mesh strainer, slotted spoon, or tongs, remove the linguine from the pots, shake off excess water, and place them in the pot with the clams. Transfer to a large bowl, toss thoroughly, garnish with the bread crumbs, and serve.

MY PASTA FRESCA WITH CHERRY TOMATOES, GARLIC, AND BASIL

SERVES 18 TO 20

6 cups all-purpose flour

12 large brown eggs

8 teaspoons plus 1 cup extra virgin olive oil

4 teaspoons plus 3 tablespoons kosher salt

about 2 cups rice flour for dusting

two 1-pint containers cherry tomatoes (about 1½ pounds), cut in half

2 garlic cloves, finely chopped

1 cup (tightly packed) basil leaves, cut into ⅛-inch strips

2 teaspoons cracked black pepper

Among the members of our extended families, I've always been known for putting together a great lunch or dinner spread for large gatherings at the house on the Cape. To me, no summer table is complete without a dish of delicate homemade pasta like this one. The "sauce" consists of juicy, ripe, uncooked little tomatoes simply dressed with extra virgin olive oil and just a few other accompaniments. Served warm, it's a satisfying filler that makes kids of all ages happy.

TIMING NOTE: While it is true that making fresh pasta is somewhat time-consuming, it is not as daunting as most people tend to believe, and it is definitely very rewarding. This recipe calls for using an electric pasta maker. The pasta dough has a resting period of at least 10 minutes and up to 2 hours. If you're putting together a feast, you can make the dough in advance of some of the other prep and cooking.

1. First make the pasta: Place the flour, eggs, 8 teaspoons of the olive oil, and 4 teaspoons of the salt in the bowl of a food processor fitted with the metal blade. Pulse several times until the dough resembles medium crumbs.

2. Dust a clean, dry work surface with the rice flour. Place the dough on the surface, gather it together, and knead until it is smooth and elastic, 5 to 10 minutes. Wrap the dough in a kitchen towel or plastic wrap and set aside to rest at room temperature for at least 10 minutes and up to 2 hours.

3. Divide the dough into three equal portions and form each into a sphere with your hands. Flatten each piece of dough into a disk ½ inch thick and dust with rice flour.

4. Set the roller of an electric pasta maker at number 1. Feed each of the dough disks, one at a time, through the roller three times. Fold the ends of the dough disks to meet in the middle and press down on the middle to seal. Feed the open side of each dough disk through the roller three more times. Fold the ends to meet in the middle and press down to seal.

5. Adjust the roller of the pasta maker to number 2. Feed the open side of the dough through the roller twice. Adjust the setting to number 3. Feed the dough through the roller twice. The pasta sheets will be quite long at this point. Cut them in half and feed each half through the roller once more. Dust each sheet with rice flour and set aside to dry slightly, 10 to 15 minutes.

6. Cut the pasta sheets into fettuccine: Layer 3 of the sheets on top of one another, with a dusting of rice flour in between each layer. Roll the sheets up together loosely and then use a sharp knife to cut them into strips or ribbons ⅓ inch wide. Loosen the rolls and stretch out the ribbons on a baking sheet. Dust with more rice

flour. Cover with a slightly dampened kitchen towel to keep them from drying out and set aside at room temperature.

7. Place the tomatoes, garlic, basil, the remaining 1 cup olive oil, 1 tablespoon salt, and the pepper in a large stainless-steel mixing bowl. Toss thoroughly so that the tomatoes are evenly coated. Set aside to marinate at room temperature for 20 minutes.

8. Place the remaining 2 tablespoons salt in a large 5-quart stockpot full of water over high heat and bring to a boil. Add the pasta and cook until the noodles float to the top, 2 to 3 minutes, stirring occasionally so the noodles don't stick together. Use tongs to transfer the noodles to the bowl with the tomatoes. Add about 1 cup of the pasta cooking water to the bowl. Toss until the ingredients are well incorporated. Transfer to a large ceramic bowl and serve.

ROASTED PORK LOIN WITH PEACH ZABAGLIONE

SERVES 18 TO 20

one 8-pound pork loin, trimmed
and tied

1 tablespoon kosher salt, plus
more to taste

2 teaspoons cracked black
pepper, plus more to taste

2 large ripe peaches, peeled,
pitted, and pureed in
a blender

6 large brown egg yolks

½ cup sugar

½ cup dry white wine

1 tablespoon fresh rosemary
leaves

Zabaglione is of ancient and undetermined origins. Some credit it to a ninth-century Piemontese monk, others to the courts of the doge in Venice or the Medici in Florence. It's a light, whipped or whisked custard, whose basic ingredients are egg yolks, sugar, and some type of sweet wine, usually marsala. Zabaglione has spread throughout the culinary world in many versions, both sweet and savory. It's often served with fresh fruit (especially peaches) on the side and sometimes with the fruit mixed in. Here I've steered the zabaglione in the direction of the savory by using dry white wine, and I've incorporated peaches to serve it as a relish for the roasted pork loin. A well-prepared roast pork (*porchetta*) commands much respect in the world of Italian cooking. I liked the idea of merging a traditional roast with a modern take on one of Italy's most famous desserts, adding complexity and sophistication to create a delicious new specialty. It's a main dish, meant to be served at room temperature, and it's ideal for larger party buffet platters.

1. Preheat the oven to 400°F.

2. Place the pork loin on a rack in a roasting pan and season with the salt and pepper. Roast for 45 minutes, or until a meat thermometer inserted into the thickest part reads 145–150°F. Remove from the oven and let rest for 20 minutes.

3. Set up a double boiler over medium heat, bringing the water to a boil before placing the upper section on top. (Use a stainless-steel bowl over a saucepan if you don't have a double boiler.) Add the peach puree, egg yolks, sugar, and white wine and whisk continuously in the shape of a figure 8 so the mixture does not stick to the sides of the pan as it thickens. Cook for 8 to 10 minutes, or until the zabaglione attains a creamy consistency, with no lumps. Set aside to cool to room temperature.

4. Slice the pork loin very thin (⅛ inch thick) and arrange it on a large serving platter. Season with salt and pepper and rosemary, garnish with the peach zabaglione evenly spread over all the slices, and serve at room temperature.

SOFT-SHELL CRAB SANDWICHES WITH WATERCRESS, AIOLI, AND FINGERLING POTATO SALAD

SERVES 18 TO 20

15 soft-shell crabs, cleaned, rinsed, and patted dry

8 large brown egg whites, lightly beaten

4 cups stone-ground cornmeal

3 tablespoons grapeseed oil

1 tablespoon kosher salt

2 bunches watercress, washed, drained, and torn into 3-inch pieces

two 2-pound loaves rustic Italian bread, sliced ½ inch thick

FOR THE AIOLI

4 garlic cloves

about 1 cup olive oil

6 large brown egg yolks

¼ cup fresh lemon juice

1 cup grapeseed oil

1 tablespoon kosher salt

2 teaspoons cracked black pepper

Soft-shell crabs are one of those astounding seasonal miracles of the food world; they are actually blue crabs in the molting stage, having lost their hard shells in the spring in preparation for growing a new coat of armor for summer and fall. Their season runs from May—mythically the first full moon of that month—until September. Here, breaded and sautéed soft-shell crabs provide a salty marine crunch, and watercress brings a refreshing peppery freshwater note. Be sure to use the best rustic Italian-style bread you can find: It sets up the balance of flavors and textures. As an option, the bread can be lightly toasted. Serving the fingerling potato salad on the side makes this a complete lunch platter for outdoor summer parties.

INGREDIENT NOTE: You can buy soft-shell crabs live at the market, bring them home, and clean them yourself, or have your fishmonger do it. The crabs will keep live in the fridge for a day or two. If you bring them home already cleaned, refrigerate them immediately and cook as soon as possible.

CLEANING INSTRUCTIONS: Wash soft-shell crabs in cold water and pat dry. Using a sharp knife or scissors, trim off the front part of the head from just behind the eyes. Do not cut off the legs or pincers. Turn the crab over on its back and remove the triangular "apron." Carefully snip off or pull out the gills, which are located underneath the pointy sides of the shell. Proceed with cooking instructions or refrigerate and cook as soon as possible.

1. Preheat the oven to 350°F.

2. First make the aioli: Place the garlic cloves and olive oil in a small ovenproof dish or pan, making sure the garlic is fully submerged, and roast in the oven for 20 minutes. Remove the roasted garlic, discard the oil (or save it for salad dressing), and pat the cloves dry. Place the roasted garlic with the egg yolks and lemon juice in a blender and turn it to medium speed. Gradually pour the grapeseed oil into the blender in a steady stream and blend until fully incorporated, about 2 minutes. Add the salt and pepper. The aioli should have a mayonnaise-like consistency. If necessary, thin it by adding cold water, about 1 tablespoon at a time, while the blender is still running. Transfer the aioli to a small ceramic bowl, adjust the seasonings, cover, and store in the refrigerator until ready to use.

3. Next make the potato salad: Place a large 5-quart stockpot about two-thirds filled with water over medium-high heat. When the water comes to a boil, add the fingerling potatoes, adjust the heat to maintain a steady boil, and cook the potatoes until fork tender, about 15 minutes. Drain the potatoes and set aside to cool.

FOR THE FINGERLING POTATO SALAD

2 pounds fingerling potatoes

1 bunch scallions, finely chopped

½ cup extra virgin olive oil

2 tablespoons fresh lemon juice

1 tablespoon kosher salt

2 teaspoons cracked black pepper

4. Cut the potatoes in half and place them in a large stainless-steel mixing bowl. Add the scallions, olive oil, lemon juice, salt, and pepper. Toss until thoroughly combined. Transfer to a ceramic serving bowl and set aside at room temperature.

5. To make the crabs, set up a breading station: Place the egg white in one ceramic bowl and the cornmeal in another, next to it. Coat each soft-shell crab lightly in egg white, then dredge in the cornmeal, making sure each is uniformly covered with a thin layer of the meal.

6. Place the grapeseed oil in a large 12-inch sauté pan over medium heat. When the oil is hot, cook the crabs, 3 at a time, until lightly browned, 2 to 3 minutes per side. Transfer to a large paper towel–lined plate or platter to drain of excess oil.

7. Place a crab and several pieces of watercress between slices of bread to make sandwiches. Cut the sandwiches in half and arrange them on a large platter. Serve with the aioli and potato salad on the side.

GRILLED SAUSAGES WITH MACERATED STONE FRUITS AND ROSEMARY

SERVES 18 TO 20

1 pound ripe peaches, washed, pitted, and cut into 2-inch wedges

1 pound ripe plums, washed, pitted, and cut into 2-inch wedges

1 pound ripe apricots, washed, pitted, and cut into 2-inch wedges

3 fresh rosemary sprigs

½ cup extra virgin olive oil

¼ cup balsamic vinegar

1 tablespoon kosher salt, plus more to taste

2 teaspoons cracked black pepper, plus more to taste

5 pounds sweet Italian sausage

This recipe makes me crave those summer cookouts on the back patio with friends and family. It offers a sophisticated twist yet is quick and easy, allowing you to enjoy a glass of prosecco while working the grill.

TIMING NOTE: The fruit needs to macerate in the fridge for 3 hours and then be removed in enough time to come back to room temperature.

1. Place the peaches, plums, apricots, and rosemary sprigs in a large nonreactive bowl. Add the olive oil, balsamic vinegar, salt, and pepper, and toss thoroughly. Cover the bowl with plastic wrap and place in the refrigerator for 3 hours. The fruit should absorb about half of the liquid. Remove the fruit from the fridge and allow time to come to room temperature, about 30 minutes. Adjust the seasonings.

2. Prepare an outdoor grill with a high heat source. Position the grilling rack 12 inches from the fire or flame.

3. Place the sausages on the grill with ample space between them (at least ½ inch) and grill until they are browned all over and their juices run clear, 2 to 3 minutes per side.

4. Transfer the sausages to a large platter, put the macerated fruit on top, and bring to the table hot.

GRILLED SKIRT STEAK PIZZAIOLA WITH SAUTÉED SPINACH AND PRESERVED LEMON

SERVES 18 TO 20

two 5-pound skirt steaks

3 tablespoons olive oil

3 garlic cloves, roughly chopped

3 lemons

4 tablespoons grapeseed oil

¼ cup (lightly packed) fresh
    oregano, chopped

pinch of red pepper flakes

one 28-ounce can whole San
    Marzano tomatoes

2 teaspoons kosher salt

½ teaspoon cracked black
    pepper

2 pounds fresh spinach leaves,
    cleaned and dried

¼ chopped preserved lemons for
    garnish (page 133)

I was first exposed to this typical Tuscan dish when we were working in Florence. Tuscany and its inhabitants are well known for their devotion to high-quality beef. Meat from the ancient Chianina breed, raised in central Italy since before Roman times, is the basis for not only the world-famous *bistecca alla Fiorentina* (Florentine-style porterhouse steak) but also many other local beef and steak preparations such as *pizzaiola*, which means "pizza style," and features a hearty pizza-style topping that stands up to and enhances the flavors of the beef. Steak *pizzaiola* is usually made with sirloin, but I've always loved skirt steak, and that's what I use. It's a relatively inexpensive, underused, and very tasty cut that lends itself well to grilling. It's also tougher, so it does need to be marinated. This is my adaptation of the *bistecca alla pizzaiola* I remember so fondly from my days learning how to cook the Tuscan way. It's particularly well suited to outdoor parties, barbecues, and other large, festive family-style gatherings.

TIMING NOTE: The steak is marinated for at least 8 hours in advance. Take out of the fridge at least 30 minutes before grilling.

1. Place the skirt steaks in 1 or 2 large glass or ceramic baking dishes or resealable plastic bags. Combine the olive oil and one-third of the chopped garlic in a small bowl and mix well. Pour the garlic-oil mixture over the skirt steaks, then squeeze the juice from 2 of the lemons over them. Turn the skirt steaks over twice to coat them thoroughly in the marinade. Cover the dish(es) with plastic wrap or seal the bag(s). Place in the refrigerator and let marinate for at least 8 hours.

2. Place 2 tablespoons of the grapeseed oil, one-third of the remaining garlic, the oregano, and red pepper flakes in a 10-inch skillet. Place over medium heat. After 1 minute, crush each tomato by hand into the pan. After all the tomatoes have been added, pour the liquid from the can into the pan and cook for 5 minutes, stirring occasionally with a wooden spoon. The consistency of the sauce should be somewhat thick, like that of a pizza sauce. Season with 1 teaspoon of the salt and ¼ teaspoon of the pepper. Remove the pan from the heat and set aside.

3. Place the remaining 2 tablespoons grapeseed oil and the remaining garlic in a 10-inch skillet. Place over medium heat and sauté. Add the spinach to the pan, one handful at a time. Shake the pan and sauté the spinach until it is completely wilted, 3 to 5 minutes. Remove the pan from the heat, squeeze the juice of the remaining lemon over the spinach, and season with the remaining 1 teaspoon salt and ¼ teaspoon pepper. Set aside.

4. Take the steak out of the fridge at least 30 minutes prior to cooking and remove it from the marinade (leaving any excess on the steak). Prepare an outdoor grill with a high heat source. Position the grilling rack 6 inches from the fire or flame.

5. For medium-rare, grill the steak 4 to 5 minutes per side. Transfer to a cutting board and let rest for about 2 minutes before cutting. Slice the steak with the grain of the meat, about $1/8$ inch thick or as thin as possible. Place over a bed of the sautéed spinach on a large platter. Place the tomato sauce on top of the sliced meat, garnish with the preserved lemon, and serve.

MERINGUES WITH POACHED SEASONAL FRUIT AND VANILLA GELATO

SERVES 18

MERINGUES

6 large brown egg whites

½ teaspoon kosher salt

1½ cups sugar

2 tablespoons cornstarch

1 teaspoon fresh lemon juice

1 teaspoon pure vanilla extract

1 teaspoon orange blossom water

zest of 1 lemon

Strolling through some of the great cities of Italy, you might find stacks of meringues piled high in the windows of local pasticcerie. They look like beautiful silky clouds, floating in the windows—and they're just waiting to be eaten. We often had an abundance of egg whites in our restaurant kitchens, and both Colleen and I would always try to devise interesting traditional uses for them. While I might offer an entrée of orata under a salt crust—the "cement" of which is egg whites—Colleen might think of ways to incorporate those Italian meringues in her dessert menu. Italians tend to like desserts that are not all about sweetness, but rather focus on flavor and texture. Especially for larger parties, keeping it simple by offering a meringue with seasonal fruit and a scoop of gelato is a great way to cleanse the palate and end a meal on a not-too-sweet note.

INGREDIENT NOTES: Your eggs should be farm-fresh; even if they're store-bought, make sure you go for the highest quality all-natural or organic. Your honey should be local. As for the type, it's really a matter of personal preference. Colleen prefers a mild honey, nothing strong like buckwheat, for this recipe. If you like a little lavender flavor, though, go for it. The orange blossom water is optional but it adds a really nice flavor accent. It's readily available at Middle Eastern and Indian specialty stores.

TIMING NOTE: The meringues are relatively quick to prepare but they do require 1½ hours baking time and a 4-hour drying period in the oven afterwards. They can be prepared well in advance and kept in an airtight container for up to 24 hours. The fruit can also be prepared a day in advance and stored in the fridge until ready to serve.

1. Preheat the oven to 180°F. Line two 9 x 13-inch baking pans with parchment paper.

2. Place the egg whites and salt in the bowl of an electric mixer with the whisk attachment, and beat at medium-high speed until frothy, about 1 minute. Reduce the speed to medium and gradually add the sugar. Increase the speed to high and beat until the mixture is firm and glossy, about 2 minutes.

3. Remove the bowl from the mixer and sift the cornstarch into the egg whites, folding them together with a rubber spatula. Add the lemon juice, vanilla extract, orange blossom water, and lemon zest, again folding them together with a rubber spatula.

4. Using a large stainless-steel spoon, place 18 equal portions of the meringue in circular mounds evenly spaced on the prepared pans. Use the back of the spoon to form a well in the top of each meringue.

5. Bake for 1½ hours. Turn off the heat and, with the door still closed, let the meringues to dry in the oven for about 4 hours. They should be hard and dry on the outside, soft and chewy inside.

Poached Seasonal Fruit

½ cup sugar

½ cup honey

1 cup dry rosé wine

½ cup water

1 teaspoon crushed aniseed

1 cinnamon stick

2 large basil leaves

8 large ripe figs

1 pint raspberries

1 pint blueberries

2 teaspoons orange blossom
    water, optional

1 tablespoon fresh lemon juice

1. Place the sugar, honey, rosé, water, aniseed, cinnamon, and basil leaves in a saucepan over medium-high heat. Bring to a boil, stirring to combine until the sugar dissolves.

2. Cut the figs in half, trim off and discard their stems. Place the figs, raspberries, and blueberries in a large bowl. Pour the hot syrup over the fruit. Stir in the orange blossom water, if using, and let cool to room temperature.

3. Add the lemon juice, cover, and refrigerate until well chilled or overnight.

To Assemble and Serve

2 quarts vanilla gelato (page 40)

36 fresh mint leaves

2 teaspoons sea salt

1. About 15 minutes before serving, remove the gelato from the freezer to soften.

2. Place the meringues in shallow bowls. Place one generous scoop of softened gelato in the well of each meringue, making an indentation in each portion of gelato to allow the fruit to pool into it. Spoon an equal portion of fruit, with juices, onto each serving of gelato. Garnish each with two mint leaves and a pinch of sea salt.

SOURCES

www.allfreshseafood.com
For seafood.

www.bowerykitchens.com
A good source for kitchen equipment, such as hand-crank pasta makers, food mills, skillets, baking sheets, and dishes, casseroles, wire-mesh strainers, and skimmers.

www.buonitalia.com
Offers high-quality imported groceries, including my favorite brand of dry pasta Setaro, fregola, amaretti, balsamic vinegar, extra virgin olive oil, risotto rice, and mascarpone.

www.chefswarehouse.com
For grapeseed oil, flour, nuts, dried fruit, ricotta, anchovies, San Marzano tomatoes, kosher salt, goat milk, and cornmeal.

www.dartagnan.com
For rabbit, pheasant, and other game meats.

www.dipaloselects.com
For meats, cheeses, and other imported Italian specialties.

www.formaggiokitchen.com
For cheeses, including mozzarella di bufala, Parmigiano-Reggiano, pecorino Romano, and ricotta.

www.gustiamo.com
High-quality imported Italian groceries, including capers, lentils, and chick peas.

www.palmbayimports.com
A wine importer, whose website includes my favorite Sicilian olive oil, Planeta, and where to purchase it.

www.kalustyans.com
For orange blossom water.

www.kitchenaid.com
For electric mixers.

www.kitchenemporium.com
For hand-crank and electric pasta makers.

www.markethallfoods.com
A European-imported specialty food site, including Umbrian lentils, frégola, jarred anchovies, ventresca tuna, oils, vinegars, and more.

www.nantucketseafood.net
This is the site for Nantucket Seafoods, or contact Ted Jensen at 508-325-6345 for bay scallops, clams, lobster, and more. (Other recommended Nantucket seafood businesses include Glidden's and Sayles.)

www.salumeriabiellese.com
A New York institution for imported Italian prosciutto and other cured meats, they make it all on premises, including guanciale, dry sausages, cacciatorini, pancetta, and soppressata. Similar outlets are Alma Gourmet (in Long Island City, Queens) and Salumeria Italiana (in Boston's North End).

www.starwest-botanicals.com
For orange blossom water.

INDEX

Page numbers in *italics* indicate illustrations

ACKNOWLEDGMENTS

There are so many people to whom I'm most grateful for helping me realize the concept of this book. I don't know if there is a table big enough to seat everyone!

First and foremost, I want to thank my own family: Colleen, Vivian, Marcella, and Roman.

Thanks to my mom and dad, Valerie and Ron Suhanosky Sr., as well as my grandmothers, Rachel Gaudino and Irene Suhanosky, and my great grandmother Rose Carbone. They gave me so many great memories of family meals around the tables profiled in this book.

Thanks to my extended family for opening up their homes, allowing me to cook in their kitchens and helping me create unforgettable dining experiences. Thank you, John and Carol Marnell. Thank you, Jen and Tom Hawkins. It's been a pleasure sharing your passion for life and love of food. A special thanks to David and Barbara Hawkins, for so many opportunities to enjoy their Cape House, which inspired the summer meals in the Alfresco chapter.

For believing in me endlessly and helping me cement the foundation of this book, I give many thanks to Megan Milner-Evans, Celeste Fine, and Anja Schmidt. I am also very grateful to the James Beard Foundation for recognizing *Pasta Sfoglia* with an award, which led to this project.

I have many words to say, but putting them in their right place is no easy task. Thanks to David Gibbons for his help with this.

Thank you Roy Finamore and Rebecca Jurkevich, for making my food photogenic for our Italian photographer Alberto Peroli.

Thank you to Winston Flowers and Be Our Guest Rentals for their support with the holiday and alfresco chapters. And thank you to Sarah Scales for helping style our kids.

Thank you to KJAB for his support throughout this process and for letting me speak my mind. A big thank you to my newfound family at Stuzzicheria. Thank you, Gerard and Carolyn Renny, for being open to my crazy ideas. Thank you, Mitch Mosallem, for believing in me.

Finally, I want to offer thanks to everyone who believes in what I do and joins me at my tables.

21 Ropa al Pompadosa
27 Cauliflower
37 Chicken al Mattone
38 Lemon Risotto
49 Pizza Rustica
55 Classic Ribollita
58 lettuce wedge w gorgonzola
72 Gnussels
75 Shaved Celery
97 Classic polpettine
98 Creamy Polenta
123 Sicilian Caponata